Unstoppable

IN THE FACE OF NO AGREEMENT

FACING OBSTACLES AGAINST ALL ODDS

STACY A. HOGG

ISBN-13: 978-1973887379
ISBN-10: 1973887371

Editor: Stacey Debono / sdebonoediting@gmail.com
Cover Design: Stacey Debono
Cover Photo by MooD-ology Photography
www.moodologyphotography.com
Facebook – MooD-ology Photography
Instagram & Twitter - moodologist

Cover Photo Clothing styled by Spoiled Boutique
www.spoiledboutique.com
Facebook - Spoiled Boutique
Instagram - spoiledboutique

Cover Photo Hair by -XO Hair Alternatives FB- xohairalternatives
Instagram - Xo_hairalternatives

Cover Photo Makeup by Yolande' Denise
www.yolandadenise@mac.com
Facebook – Yolande'Denise
Instagram - Yolande'Denise

Official Website: www.stacyaudriene.com
Facebook - stacyaudriene
Instagram- stacy_audriene
Twitter- stacyaudriene

This book is dedicated to....

Mother. *Mama I DID IT. I became the women you raised me to be. When you left this earth you blessed my life and told me everything I touched was going to turn into gold. Even when I fell I somehow held on to those words. You were not here to see me fall, but you were the WIND BENEATH MY WINGS as I got back up.*

Daddy. *Thank you for validating me before you left this earth too, you told me to run with my music sound, and to be OK with the fact that I don't sound like any other artist. You and mama are not here to see the outcome but even you told me that I would be fine and I am!*

Sedric Gadson. *When I started this book project you were right here with me. Your untimely death took a great toll on my life and my journey to finish this book. Your spirit will live on through the music portion of this book, and I will forever tell your children how much they were loved by you.*

Isaiah & Gladys Randolph. *You both were the best grandparents in the whole wide world. You were there to help my mother raise us when life got rough. Grandma thank you for nurturing my love for hair styling and hair care. You were the best mentor ever! And I deserved every whooping you gave me!*

Richard & Velva Hogg. *Thank you both for being our safe haven. Weekends with you were absolutely fun! I know that I was the challenging grand-kid and I wish that you both were here to see the women I became today. I will forever hold on to your teachings and values.*

INTRODUCTION

I wrote this book to share with you, my readers, that which I know and now live by. This book incorporates portions of my life experiences, from a child well into my adult years. I realized early on in my journey that it is not about what you go through, it is about how you come out of it.

I was at a point in my life where I was stuck, and told myself that something had to change. It may be something that is not working in our life or not working as well as we want it to, but that is OK. Our trials and misfortunes come to build character, that is how we grow. I felt that it was important to share my story with you simply because I haven't always lived my life as a perfect role model, and I am not afraid to tell from where God brought me. I did not fix my life on my own; I was headed for destruction and God saved me. There is no other way to describe it. Silence is impossible for the true believer when your life has transformed. You cannot be silent.

Someone needed to hear my story and the testimony of where God has brought me; I am a living proof. If he did it for me, he will do it for you. I had to say, "Lord, here I am a sinner, save me and forgive me." I surrendered, and then He lifted me up. Nothing I ever did was hidden from Him. He uncovered everything I have ever done.

We all have had some type of dysfunction in our homes, we all stumble in life, and we all want the same basic things in life. We just have to take different journeys. Yes, we may stumble in the journey, but when we get back up we are armed with strength (1samuels2:4).

I close this book by sharing with you the steps I took in being unstoppable. I put in day-to-day work to keep myself grounded. With every molecule of life in me, I declare that whoever needs to hear my story will pick up this book and

1

soundtrack, and be blessed by it and share it. I pray that every reader is touched, moved and inspired to be unstoppable!

I
WHAT SHAPED ME

My grandparents, Isaiah and Gladys Randolph, moved to Oakland, California in 1946. My grandfather was in the Navy, stationed at Treasure Island in San Francisco. After discharging from the Navy, he sent for my grandmother and my uncle so that they could live the American dream. He had dreams and hope. They were destined for a better life; he discovered a place where there was no segregation, unlike the state of Louisiana. My grandfather knew that there was a better life in California, and he moved with faith that he could create a better life for his family. They lived with family members who had already been in Oakland until they bought their first home in West Oakland. My grandmother worked in the shipyard while going to beauty school. She finished beauty school and received her license on April 3, 1946. My grandfather had the downstairs basement remodeled and my grandmother opened her hair salon "Style Rite Beauty Salon", a family salon. My grandmother operated her business with love. Women brought their whole family to get their hair done at her shop.

Members of our family were constantly migrating from Louisiana; my grandparent's house during this time was almost like a family hostel. Family from Louisiana and Texas moved to Oakland and started their journey at my grandparent's house. They stayed there until they found stable work and a place of their own. This was during the time when black people helped each other and had compassion for one another.

Five years later, on May 21 1954, my mother was born. My grandmother had a miscarriage before my mother was born so they called her "The Miracle Child". When my mom was born, she was in the breech position and the doctors had to turn her around for delivery. Somehow they broke her arms in the process, but this didn't stop her from what would be her life – playing the piano like my grandfather. She was born a musician and had love for the piano; she started playing the piano and organ at 10 years old and by the time she was 14, she had her first job at a local church in West Oakland.

My parents met at church and they went to school together at Castlemont High School. They eventually got married; my mother was sixteen, my father was eighteen. Their wedding was a "shot gun wedding"; my mother was three months pregnant and my grandmother was not settling for an abortion. She forced my parents to get married before the baby was born. My dad's parents and my mother's parents were very active in the church and they were concerned about what having children that were unmarried teenage parents would look like to others. Back then, there was no question - if you got a girl pregnant, you had to marry her.

***

December 3, 1970. My sister Sherron was born, and for teenage parents, they had their business together. They had a condominium by Lake Merritt, a nice part of town. My dad had his job and life was grand. However, their marriage was going downhill, and times became rough for my mother. Dad's addiction to alcohol became worse, which negatively affected their marriage and he became physically abusive. He was on his way to college when my mother got pregnant, but all of that came to a halt when he had to marry her and become a family man. He made the decision to do the right thing and marry my mother; my grandmother Gladys had a lot of influence on his decision, but he did it with resentment which was evident by the way he treated my mother. Dad was causing a ruckus. By the time I was born two years and nine months later, the drinking had gotten worse and my sister recalls my father in a argument with my mother when I was born and my father had picked me up from my crib and threw me across the room in a drunken rage.

My earliest memory of my father was the Oakland Police Department (OPD) throwing him down several flights of stairs after he and his cousin stabbed my aunt. My aunt had thrown a birthday party for my mother, and my dad and his cousin Ronnie crashed it...to say the least.

4

My mother hung in there for as long as she could; she didn't believe in getting divorced. She did everything to try to help my father and save their marriage. But it was not getting better; my father finally beat her to the point where she had to be hospitalized; my grandparents could not recognize her. She knew after this that things were not going to get any better and she put a plan of action together.

Mama told me that she left him to protect not only herself but my sister and I as well. She did not want us to grow up thinking that it was normal to be hit on and abused by a man. Somehow through the grace of God she pulled herself up by the boot straps and courageously walked away from that marriage with two babies and just the clothes on her back; she left everything. My mother had been beaten beyond recognition and my grandparents stepped in; my mother knew it was never going to stop because it got worse each time.

She was a musician to the bone. She always had a job playing for the church while working as a collection agent and receptionist. Getting on her feet was a struggle, and my sister and I were her little soldiers. My mother taught us to work as a team and to always stick together.

***

1977. Four years had passed, and my father was in a new relationship and had my youngest sister, Sabrina, born on November 29th of that year. Sherron and I were excited to have a little sister, but we didn't see her a lot. We saw her only when we went to visit my dad on the weekends. My mother suffered even more because now he had three kids to feed. Throughout our childhood years, he did little to support us financially and emotionally. My grandmother would do for us in his name on the holidays. She would buy us things and say that it was from him on Christmas. He had top of the line benefits for us and he spent the court ordered time with us, but emotionally he was not there for us or himself. How could he be there for us? My father never told me I was beautiful or validated me in any type of way. I was always looking for him to be there to support me when I performed in

5

talent shows and plays, but he never was. At that time the relationship between my mother and father was very toxic. The divorce proceedings made it that way, I'm sure.

After the divorce was final, we would call him and ask him for new shoes or extra spending money. He would always tell us 'no' or his famous quote, "They already taking that money out my check." which was only fifty dollars per child, per month. It got to the point where my sister and I would say it with him simultaneously when we asked for anything. Dad was so bitter about having to pay child support that he would not help my mother with clothes and school supplies. I grew up with many hand-me-downs from my sister, toys included. If it was not for my grandparents helping out, I don't know where we would have been. We had no idea that we were a heartbeat away from a cardboard box. Mama made life seem fun and adventurous; I remember more fun times than bad.

We had a village that raised us. My great aunt Mary and Aunty Gwen, and my mother's first cousins Sharon, Debra, and Cathy, had us all the time. We would also be at Aunty Mildred's house where we spent a lot of time with our cousins Karen, Lisa, and Rachelle, who would watch us too. We were there more than enough; whenever my mother had a gig or traveled, we were always with family so being without my mom when she was traveling doing music there was never a dead space. My sister and I had a great childhood. Mildred was my grandmother's niece. Her house was one of our safe havens because she loved us like she loved her own children. I always say your family members are the first people you encounter in life, and they are the blueprint of what your perception of life is. I was bullied by my cousins and we fought, but I loved all of them to life.

Our whole family went to Mt. Zion Baptist Church, a well respected church in Oakland. Most Sundays all of our family would be at church, and my cousins would pick me up from Sunday school. They would take me to the ladies room and make me fight the other little girls at church; it got so bad that I started fighting boys too. I learned this behavior from the older kids I was around. I was not afraid of anything, and I loved playing with the

6

boys; I was a tomboy. One summer at Vacation Bible School I was fighting a boy and they called me into the church to pray for me. After the church mothers prayed with me, I went right out and beat the boy up again. Those church mothers never forgot; Sister Wright had Alzheimer's disease and could still tell that story like it was yesterday. I was not afraid to fight at all and she reminded me of it every time I saw her. I was the kid that if you got too close to in a threatening way, I was going to get you out of my face quickly!

***

Belle Vista Elementary, September 1978. I started kindergarten, and I remember being so excited to be going to school. Later that year I was bullied and I'd come out swinging on whoever looked like they were coming my way. I never knew why the girls wanted to fight me or were mean to me. I vividly remember two girls saying that they were going to fight me after school; I had never fought, and for the first time it was with two at one time. After school they ganged up on me and had me backed up against the wall, literally. I had on a belt that day and all I could think to do was to take off my belt and start swinging. I did not stop swinging until they backed up. A yard duty teacher resolved the issue but from that point forward, I owned a distorted reality that I had to fight, and I owned this well into my teenage and young adult years. I was also teased for my last name. I hated roll call; I would say HERE! as soon as I heard the teachers say 'Stacy'. This worked for some teachers but not all of them. At an early age, I began to pick up insecurities regarding my identity.

My parents' divorce was final and by this time they had established custody; my father had us on the weekends. My sister and I would love to go to his house - he loved to party, and he would play his stereo so loud but the neighbors would never complain. They knew it was the weekend and Morris was having his own private party. Later that year my mother went to Japan for nine months with her group, "The Nine Lives". The band consisted of eight men and my mother was the ninth. Before they left for Japan, my mother would have to rehearse at least three nights a week. She would get us ready for bed and take us to the rehearsal studio for hours. The band was a Top 40 band; they sang a lot of O'Jays and Heatwave tunes. This became a huge part of our lives as well because it took a lot of my mother's time, and because she had no sitter. My sister and I were right there with her at rehearsals.

By the time the group left for Japan, my sister and I were back in school from summer vacation, and my grandmother took care of us while she was gone. She was a very religious woman and did not really like the fact that my mother was playing secular music; she gave my mother a hard time about leaving us to go play "worldly music". My grandmother was old school and didn't understand that my mother had a love for all kinds of music; she complained but ended up keeping us anyway for the nine months my mother was gone.

During that nine month period, my mother would write us from Japan and tell my sister to teach me how to read and write. Growing up, my sister was almost like a mama to me. I don't remember life without her. She taught me everything I knew. I would always wait for her to answer first when my mom would ask us anything. "Where do you want to eat?" I would look to Sherron to see what answer she was going to give. My mother got hip to this and would ask me first, but I still looked to my sister. My mother tried to break this before she left but it didn't work; to this day, I still look to my sister for advise.

I missed my mother so much. Even though she wrote us often, it was not the same as her being there. During that time, my father would come get us on weekends and we would have lots of fun; we would go fishing and bowling, and he would always take us to his cousin Ronnie's house. Ronnie's girlfriend Shirley was a village parent, and whenever my dad and his cousin were over their alcohol limit for driving, we would end up having to spend the night. Those weekends we never went home; she would not let him drive drunk with my sister and I in the car. We spent a lot of time there playing with my extended family, Karen and Edward. I remember they had a stereo system that had a dome light attached to a microphone. We would all perform, and I started really

8

enjoying it, I actually enjoyed people watching me sing. I had only been used to singing in the kids choir, but I didn't get the same feeling singing in the choir. I begged my dad for one of those stereos but he never got it. I do not think he knew or could even recognize that I wanted to sing. My grandparents would come get us and take us camping at Yosemite and to Disneyland in Anaheim in the family motor home. I loved it! My sister and I had road names; she was Big S and I was Little S. We would talk on CB's with other people who would be caravanning with us on the road.

My grandmother Gladys nurtured my passion and love for hair styling. She would pick me up from preschool and take me back to the salon with her to work. At the age of five, I was into the latest soap opera series and had picked up old school salon habits. Every day in the salon for nine months I had no choice but to pass time by emulating my grandmother. I stayed in trouble; I would bring my Barbie dolls to the shop and use real shampoo on their hair. This is where my love for doing hair was created. I started out standing on a crate to shampoo my sister's hair since I was not tall enough to reach the shampoo bowl. I was only 5 and was all ready to move to the next step, which was blow drying and pressing. I think by the time I was 7 I started pressing hair on a mannequin. She taught me how to hold the shampoo nozzle without spraying water everywhere, and people used to take pictures of me at the shampoo bowl out of disbelief that a 5 year old was actually standing on a crate shampooing clients like an adult.

My mother's tour in Japan was finally over and I could not wait to see her. I remember when she got off that plane she was so pale; she looked like a white woman and I didn't recognize her. Her face was so light; I guess it was from that good eating. She had a great big bag on rollers with gifts for me and my sister. We were one of the first kids with Hello Kitty dolls and accessories right from Japan! We did not know what we had. She brought us lots of Yin, and clothes too. I really didn't care about none of that stuff though; I was just happy to have my mother home.

We stayed with my grandmother when she came home from Japan as my mother needed time to find us another place to live. When she left for Japan she had to let our place go; it didn't make sense to pay rent for a place we weren't going to occupy. After coming back, Mother decided to go to music college, and she applied to Berklee College of Music in Boston. She was accepted and we were on our way to live in Boston, Massachusetts . She left before my sister and I to get things set up before we came out to Boston. Here we were again without my mother. It was not so bad, though, because we knew that she would be back to get us in two months.

When she came back to take us to Boston, we caught the Amtrak train. It was so fun; the trip was three days long and it was the best three days of my life. We made the best of the situation; it was a long train ride and my sister and I were restless, but my mother had a way of making any situation fun. One night we ate dinner in the restaurant on the train, and after dinner my sister and I had to use the bathroom. There was only one stall and a sitting room. My mother made us sit down and she went into the bathroom stall. When she came out she was fully naked! She started singing, "Too Many Fish in the Sea". *"Listen here girls, and take this advise always in life..."* I thought that was the funniest thing ever. Our three day Amtrak trip did not seem long at all; as a matter of fact, it wasn't long enough! We finally got to Boston and Mama took us to our new home.

***

3 Fendale Ave., Dorchester, Massachusetts. 1979. This was our new address in Boston. We were now growing up in a metropolitan white neighborhood and it was different; the buildings, the people, subway trains, everything. I was so happy that it was snowing, I couldn't believe it. I was just a little city girl from California where it never snowed unless we went to the mountains, so it was exciting to live and play in the snow.

After about a month though, I was over it. We couldn't get out of the house some days without shoveling snow out of the driveway, not to mention my mother would bundle us up so tight and warm for school that my sister and I looked like little walking penguins because we had so many layers of clothes on.

10

We moved in with a lady named Mary. She opened her doors to us until my mother found us a place of our own. Mary was so nice. She played with my sister and me all the time. She didn't have any kids of her own, so she enjoyed spending time with us.

Things seemed to be going well. My mother had a part-time job while attending Berklee College of Music, and my sister and I were in school. I hated being the new girl all the time, having to meet new friends and starting all over again. I had already been to two different elementary schools and now I was at my third in Boston. I remember feeling so nervous and scared that the kids were going to tease me about my name, call me different names, and not see me for me. I felt like instead, they would see this black child that looked different from everyone else. I spent so much time trying to get comfortable in my own skin, getting comfortable with my own name, being unique, and being black and different.

We went to the Endicott School, where we had to sit in our desk with correct posture and our hands folded in front of us. This was so different from any school I had attended back in California. When we went out for recess, we had to form a line and go to the restroom before playing. There were teachers in there that handed you soap and a towel to dry your hands, sort of like when you're at a club or venue and the lady attendants in the bathroom handed you towels; the only difference was we didn't have to pay them.

The school also incorporated paddling. I'm not telling you what I heard, I'm telling you what I know and I was paddled often. It seemed as though I got paddled twice a week for minor things like forgetting homework and talking in class. This type of school taught us posture and discipline and we were under very strict rules. There was not a heavy black population at our school in Boston where we lived, and I had to work a little harder than other kids in my class. The teacher would not call on me if I wasn't sitting straight up, chest out, and head up. That was the rule for everyone but for some reason I felt like I wasn't good enough because she never called on me. I always strove to be the teacher's helper, so every time the opportunity knocked I made sure to be in position to get the job. This was my first experience in feeling like I had to do more and go over and beyond to get recognized. I never gave up, and I didn't get discouraged. One day the teacher said, "Who wants to take the attendance to the office?" I didn't raise my hand. I immediately sat up straight, chest out, and head up! The teacher looked around the room, and said "Stacy". My whole face lit up! Finally she had called on me. I thought, "Wow, never give up!" After all those no's, I finally got a yes and I didn't stop believing.

We had been there two months, and it didn't take my mother long to meet new friends with her bubbly personality. She and Mary had a friend named Cornbread; he owned an aquarium downtown called Cornbread's Aquarium. Since my mother was in school and working, she needed another village to help with us: the Wilson family, my godparents Clayton & Barbra, and my cousin Brenda. Being from California, I imagine it was really hard for her to let us loose and in the care of others, but she did what she had to do. She taught us how to catch the subway to Cornbread's Aquarium after school when she had to work or got out of class late. My sister would read the signs and off we went, commuting at an early age. Cornbread had two daughters of his own and we became close to them. They were like our big sisters; we went everywhere with them. We missed our own family, so connecting and making extended family was very easy.

Mama later met a man named Willie Lee Gadson. He spoiled me and my sister to death; he would take us to a toy store and let us get whatever we wanted. Boy, did he know how to reel us in. We got sleighs for the snow and more. He started coming around quite often to take us places and spend time with my mother; we got used to him being around.

After about six months things got pretty ugly between my mother and Mary. I still don't know to this day what happened. All I know is that we packed our things and went to live in what looked like an apartment building with *Salvation Army* written on it. The only time I had seen the Salvation Army was when my grandmother would make donations to people in need and it didn't look like that building so I could only wonder why the apartment building was called "Salvation Army".

When we got inside, there was a big kitchen and rooms; I thought we were going to have our own room until my mother broke the bad news. We were all going to reside in just one room; we were living in a shelter for women. I never knew that it was a shelter until my mother told me twenty years later. My mother remained in good spirits the whole time. If she was depressed we never knew it. We started attending the church downstairs every Sunday and soon after that mama started playing for a church across town.

One Sunday we were walking home from church and my mother stopped to throw up. I remember feeling so sad for my mother. "Mama, are you all right?" "Yes, Stacy," she replied. Soon after, Mama told us that she was pregnant. My sister and I knew it was by Willie because they were seeing a lot of each other; my sister and I were grown and always in grown folks' business.

About five months passed and mama's stomach was getting bigger. The church bought her tons of maternity clothes and some shoes. My sister and I were excited because we were going to have a new sister or brother.

Apparently, our time was up at the Salvation Army and Mama started looking for a place to stay. She eventually found a place but my sister and I were not going to occupy the new place with her. My grandmother made her send us back to California because she didn't want my mother struggling with us. That's what grandparents did back in the day - they helped take up the slack and did not let her struggle with three babies.

Before we left she made us swear that we would not tell anyone that she was pregnant. The next week we were on a 747 back to California by ourselves. That was so fun. We got all the attention on the plane since we were little girls and flying without an adult. When we got back to Oakland, we did not say anything about my mother being pregnant; we held my mother's secret like soldiers! We were sworn to secrecy. I do not remember Mama telling us when she was coming back home to California but it didn't matter because we were going back to my grandparents house which was the only home we knew. We were spoiled!

Four months later, on October 29, 1980, my mother called and told us the good news. We had a baby brother and she asked what we should name him. Sherron suggested 'Sedric' with an "S" so we all of our names would start with an S, and I suggested Devon. My mother named him Sedric Devon Gadson.

Later in my adult years, my mother told us that she was going to put my brother up for adoption because she could not see herself being a mother of three on her own. She didn't believe in abortions and felt like his life deserved a chance. When he was born the adoptive family came to pick him up and she lost it! She had a breakdown and told the adoption agency that she could not give up her only son. She changed her mind about giving him up the day he was born. The family had come to the hospital to get him and she had a fit. She said that because he was a boy and her only son, she just could not do it.

George Meeks, her friend from years prior, came to Boston when she had my brother so that he could drive mom home back to California. When my mother arrived at my grandparent's house, she had Sedric bundled up in her arms. We could not wait to see him. He had little baby hives on his face and curly hair. He was the cutest little boy; people would often ask if he was a girl. We stayed with my grandparents until Mama was able to get on her feet, get a job, and take care of us.

Eventually that living situation came to an end because my mother and grandmother had lots of arguments over God knows what. By the time my brother was six months old, he was pulling pots and pans out of the cabinet and beating on them with spoons. It was so funny to see him play with the pots and pans because in his mind he heard music that we didn't hear. My grandmother bought him his first set of drums when he turned one.

We finally moved two years later to an apartment in East Oakland, not far from our school, Burbank Elementary. We had to catch the bus to school every morning and take my brother to daycare which was about five or six blocks from our school. My sister and I were still commuters but this time with a baby. We had it all together; when the bus got to our stop I would grab the bottom of his stroller, my sister would grab the handles and we picked him up to load him onto the bus. People would look at us like "I know this is not their child!". We got to school on time every day. My sister and I, especially my sister, had a lot of responsibility at an early age. We would have to pick him up after school as well, and sometimes get dinner started. I was the middle child so I was caught in the middle - too young to get dinner started and too old to just sit around and do nothing. I always found peace combing my Barbie doll's hair and playing dress up. I always found peace in styling hair; that was my safe haven.

Four years later my brother's father, Willie, asked my mother to marry him and off to South Carolina we went. I was not excited to be moving to the South. We drove from California to South Carolina listening to Prince's *Purple Rain* album. It had just dropped and my sister and I were avid Prince fans. We had Prince posters that we had to beg to put up while living at my grandmother's house. She didn't want posters of half naked men hanging up in our room. We had the album, the tape, and if CD's were out then we would have had that, too! I knew every song on that album from beginning to end. Listening to some of those lyrics as an adult I wonder why we didn't get in trouble for singing them. Songs like Darling Nikki and Sex Shooter from Vanity 6 were lyrically risque but the melody of the songs is what always got me.

Three days turned into four; four days from California to South Carolina. My mother decided to drive her 1979 Plymouth Horizon, it was cream with a hatchback. I can't tell you how we did it but it was my sister, my brother, and I. Our cousin Lisa also came along for the ride to be company for my mom; we were packed in that car like sardines! We had bags in the hatchback, suitcases on top of the car, and bags under our feet. Most of the way my sister and I rode side by side with our feet up on each side. We had our radio with our Prince tape and life was grand! I think we actually played Prince the whole way. I remember singing and laughing the whole time. The shocks went out on Mama's car as we were traveling through Texas. We were weighed down with five people and luggage on top of the car, and when we hit a bump, the car would bounce uncontrollably and scrape. My sister and I laughed the whole time; my mother was so mad at us, and very frustrated, I'm sure. We finally went to a highway service mechanic and got back on the road.

As we got closer to South Carolina, I became withdrawn; it had dawned on me that my sister would be going back to California after the weekend. My sister and I had never been apart, so this was quite scary for me because I had always looked to her to make the decisions when we did anything; it was as if she was the boss of me. Sherron was an upwardly bound student and was going to attend Cal Berkeley that fall, and my grandmother suggested that she stay home to get the benefits of the program. I didn't understand all of that at the time. I just remember feeling that it wasn't fair that she got to go back and I had to stay in a town that looked like a scene from the movie, *The Color Purple.*

When we pulled up to what would be our new home that was built by my new stepfather, I could not believe it! There were moss trees everywhere, all the houses were made of brick, and in some areas there were communities of trailer homes. When we got out of the car, it was still hot and humid at 8pm. I could not believe the smell; it smelled like sewage mixed with green trees, it was somewhat odd. Most of the homes had ditches in front of them and there were no mountains!

The next morning my stepfather and his brothers killed a hog for us and I couldn't understand why. They said it was a "welcome to South Carolina" gesture; well, it didn't make me feel welcomed at all. I really felt sorry for the hog and felt that he had to die because of me. I know that might sound strange, but I'm a city girl. I was not ready to watch my food slaughtered right before my eyes. Knowing what I know now, I wish that I was more appreciative for having farm living experiences and being able to eat fresh food, but at 9 years old going to the grocery store seemed more civilized.

After feasting on the hog, everyone went into my stepfather's club to party and have fun. Most of my brother's family was there. They had a big family, the acres and property to go with it; it was just country as hell. I did not want my sister to leave but the time came for her and my cousin Lisa to catch their flight back to California. I cried so much; I just could not imagine life without her. I had to go to a new school without her, I had to make new friends without her, and had to make decisions without her. We always had each other so when people did not want to be our friends we would just be our own friends, and I was never lonely.

After three weeks, my mother finally enrolled me in school in Ridgeland, South Carolina. The kids found out quickly that I was the new girl from California, so that made me famous; everyone wanted to know if I knew Michael Jackson or if I had ever met Prince. I started to lie and said yes, but instead just said that I drove by Michael's house one time when I was passing Encino. I had to say something to make myself look good.

My grandmother relaxed my hair before we moved to South Carolina and after eight weeks had passed, my hair was nappier than a man's hairy chest that resembled taco meat. You could not see the parts my mother made in my hair with the ponytails, and the kids teased me on the bus every morning on the way to school. I got on at the last stop so I could never get a back seat; I had to sit in the front with my back to the kids laughing and talking about me. I hated getting on that bus; I was the butt of every joke, every morning.

I saw burning cornfields and snakes in the road while walking to the store that was three miles away. The kids taught me how to go craw fishing in the creeks. I was starting to get used to my new home. One day my brother's cousins came to the house and asked if I wanted to play. My mother was out looking for a job and my stepfather was at work. They said we were going to play hide and seek, but on a different level. They would tie me up and hide me, and I would have to seek my way out. I opted to go first, so they sat me down, blindfolded me, tied me to a chair, and picked me up. When they finally set me down, they pulled the blindfold off of me and to my surprise I was sitting right in the middle of a hog pen with four big hogs in it! I was screaming for dear life. How do I find my way out of the ropes and how am I going to walk over all this hog slop? I untied myself and reluctantly walked on top of the trash and slop to get out.

Meanwhile the boys were crackin' up because of my city girl reactions. I ran into the house and immediately took a shower, I was so grossed out! I smelled like trash; it was so nasty. Later that evening, someone told my mother that I was having sex in the hog pen and I got the whoopin' of my life! I was trying to explain to my mother that we were playing hide and seek, and she beat me more. Fortunately for me, the kids came to my rescue and assured my mother that we were only playing. I don't remember if she apologized; I was just happy they saved me.

I had a summer job picking cucumbers. The experience was amazing. I actually felt like I was in the cotton fields and I got a taste of how they survived in the country. My grandmother had always told us stories about her and her brothers in the cotton fields, so having this experience intrigued me. I had no idea that cucumbers came with thorns; the only time I saw cucumbers were in the grocery store cleaned up and smooth. My hands had welts on them from picking after a days' work. It really was not a lot of money but at the end of the day it was an experience and money for me spend. Picking cucumbers was my very first job.

Six months passed and my stepfather started acting strange; he became mean and very agitated. I would hear him and my mom arguing and I tried to listen but at the same time I drowned them out and tried to act like I didn't hear them. One evening, I heard him slap my mother during an argument. I could not take it anymore - I ran into my bathroom and took the towels off the towel holder, broke the pole off, and ran into the room and said, "If you hit my mother again I will BASH your head in!" He turned to my mom and said, "You have a disrespectful kid." I remember thinking to myself, "What's more disrespectful? You hitting a woman or the woman's child protecting her mom?" My mom had a job in Savannah, Georgia but the next day she didn't go to work. After my stepfather left for work my mother woke me up and told me that we were going back to California. I was so happy; in my 10-year-old mind I felt that we should have never gone to South Carolina anyway, but what did I know?

She went into town to handle last minute business, but before leaving she showed me how to 'army pack' by rolling our clothes into small rolls to fit all it all into the suitcase. I packed as quickly as I could because I knew that we were trying to be gone before he came home from work. My mother finally came back from running errands and I was done packing her clothes, my brother's clothes, and mine. The whole house was packed and ready to be loaded.

We packed the car and were ready to go. As we were pulling out of the driveway, my step-dad came home from work. I was so scared, I didn't know what he was going to do. My mother parked the car and went into the house with him. I was so upset because I knew he was trying to talk her into staying and I was ready to go back to California. I had already written my grandmother (my dad's mom) and told her to secretly send me a ticket to come home, I was done with country living. I wanted to come back to the city where we went to the grocery store for food and milk. I lost so much weight because I was afraid to eat. We ate chicken straight from the chicken coop, our bacon and pork chops were running around in slop, and our milk came straight from the cow; I could not deal with the country life anymore and I was ready to go. My mom came back to the car and told me we were staying. I was mad, I could not believe it. Hours later my mother came into my room and said "DO NOT UNPACK!" I knew exactly what was going on. She was pretending that we were staying; I think I slept with my clothes on that night. I wanted to be ready to hop up and be on the road, headed back to California.

The next morning we did just that. The day before was a test run obviously because when he left for work, we left too! We drove nonstop back to California. My mother was so tired on the road that she would tell me to me grab the wheel when she dosed off. I was only 10 years old, and it was exciting. Looking back, that was dangerous; she was running for dear life, and in her mind she was trying to get home and as far away from him as possible. I know for my mother it was heartbreaking; she was now divorcing again, coming out of a new marriage that had only lasted six months. She was not going to go through another abusive relationship even it was my brother's father. She was not going to subject me to that life when she had walked away from my father for the same type of behavior nine years prior. I was a baby and never saw the abuse, but this time I witnessed this behavior for myself and it was scary. It taught me a valuable lesson - never stay in an abusive relationship. It will never get better, only worse, if you stay in it.

We finally made it back to California at about 8pm on Christmas night. Most of our family was still at my grandmother's house, and I could not wait to see my big sister. When I walked into the house everyone just looked at me and asked, "Where is all of your weight?" It was that obvious that I had lost weight since we were gone. All of my cousins were there, too. I was so happy to be back in my city.

We stayed with my grandmother for about two years; by this time I was 12 years old and coming into my own. I liked boys, my Barbie dolls were becoming less interesting, and my hormones were going crazy. I met a 16 year old boy that I liked and his friend liked my sister. They would ride their bikes to our house and we would entertain them in the backyard; we were forbidden to have boys in the house, but somehow we found a way to sneak them in. That same year I lost my virginity and I hated it. I did not like the feeling, and I never explored sex again with him. I was always told "no sex before marriage" and at 12 years old I was not ready for marriage. We kept in contact, but that was it. He liked me; he didn't care that I didn't want to have sex and we remained friends but we lost contact for about four years. We then reunited and dated until I was 18. My parents had never talked to me about self worth. All my grandmother would tell me was, "No sex before marriage!" but that wasn't telling me anything.

Hold On…

Hold on don't let go
To see what happens the next day
Hold on don't let go to affirmations every day
I hold on and don't let go
To positive images, in my mind.

Sometimes it seems like it's a waste of time
What do I have to lose
Only I can choose my destiny.

Hold on and don't let go

He will never leave or forsake you
Even in your darkest hour
He will be right there

Hold on and don't let go

To this roller coaster called life.
I hold on and don't let go
To my mothers words
"Keep God first"
I hold on and don't let go
And the rest will be added.
Hold on and don't let go to gratitude
And thanks for all you have.

Hold on and don't let go

He will never leave or forsake you
Even in your darkest hour
He will be right there

Hold on and don't let go

21

II
All My Life

4320 Daisey St., Oakland, CA, 1986. We were finally in our own place again. Our apartment was on a hill with a view, and my mother was in a happy space. One morning at about 2am, my mother got a call from my uncle saying that my cousin Karen was shot and killed in front of her mother's house. They shot her while her 4 year old daughter was in the car asleep. This was my cousin that used to babysit my sister and I; she and my mom were more like sisters. My mother was devastated and went into full depression; I had never seen my mother like that. I was devastated too because I was a child trying to figure out who would want to hurt my cousin. There was so much confusion going on in my head, and our family was traumatized. We had to go through a court battle for my little cousin, and to this day we still have no justice or peace regarding her murder. Having to experience this at such a young age with someone so close to me was traumatic.

My sister and I were reaching our preteens, and we were on a drill team called The Flaming Five. We practiced once a week in Berkeley at the Elks Lodge. Our practice day was the same day that we had our weekly hair appointment with my grandmother, and we would want to get in and out. If only it were that easy.

My grandmother would tell us that we had to wait until she finished with her paying clients before she would even shampoo our hair, and that made me step up my hair game. I quickly learned how to do everything; press and curl, and style, you name it, I was doing it. We were older and did not have time to sit in the shop all day and wait. After about two months of doing hair, I began to really enjoy it, not to mention that I already had a lot of practice from years of being at the shop.

I liked doing hair so much that I told my friends to come to the shop to have their hair styled for twenty dollars. I had two clients - Marlow Holloway and Tiffany Watson. Life was grand;

this was the beginning of my making money styling hair.

Mama tried to do the best she could to give us what we needed, from a roof over our head to spiritual guidance. My mother always tried to further her knowledge in whatever it was that she did, but this time was the straw that broke the camels back. She met a guy named Bill Keener who later became her third husband. Bill was a studying Jehovah's Witness and was really adamant about converting our family from Baptists to the Kingdom Hall, and although now I feel that all knowledge of God is good, I did not see things that way at 14 years old. He came in changing things right away; he never tried to get to know my sister and me. It was like a new sheriff was in town and he was out to have his way. We could not go to family gatherings on Christmas and Thanksgiving...not to mention Mama stopped cooking with salt because he had high blood pressure! I could not believe it.

One night my mother called my dad over to the house to talk to me because I had just gotten suspended from school for fighting. When my dad got there, she was on the phone in her room with Bill. My dad was in the living room hollering and yelling at me for my behavior. Somehow Bill thought that he was yelling at my mother and came to our house to jump on my dad. My dad called him a 'salt free mutha fucka' and was about to stab him with an ice pick! My sister and I begged my dad not to kill him and he left. It was all a misunderstanding and could have been prevented. I was glad no one got hurt.

One Wednesday evening my mother told me and my sister to get ready to go to the Kingdom Hall for the first time. She jumped into the shower and told us to be ready when she got out, and boy, was I ready. I packed my clothes into a gym bag, dirty and all, and quickly ran into my sister's room and said, "I'm out! Are you coming or staying?" I did not give her much time to decide because my mother had just gotten out of the shower. The next thing I knew, my sister grabbed her clothes and we were out. As we were leaving my little brother ran to the door and said, "Take me too!" We just looked back at him and told him that we would be back for him. We were literally running away from home on foot. I was an adventurous child with my wise self, always thinking ahead. We went to a park until sundown so my mother would not find us. Little did I know she never looked for us. She later told us that when she found that we were gone she got dressed and went to the Kingdom Hall anyway. It was very scary because I did not know what to do next. All I knew was that I was free from bondage and a salt-free diet.

My mother gave us a chance to come home, but the same rules still applied if we were under her roof. We had to serve Jehovah God, which was not a problem but why no holidays? We did not go back home. I could not see how I would be able to live without being with family on holidays; I truly thought my mother had lost her mind. Little did I realize that this was a time when I really needed to be around my mother. I was heading into my teens; I thought I was grown but I needed more time to get that last bit of training before being on my own. Somehow I felt at 14 years old I was ready to conquer the world.

We moved in with my Aunt Mildred. I was a little scared because we still did not know who killed my cousin, and now I was about to live there. My sister and cousin shared a room, and I had to share a room with my great aunt who was suffering from Alzheimer's. I remember sleeping in the room with her and looking over at her to make sure she was still alive. She was in her final stages and slept a lot; it was a very scary situation for me. I didn't want to be in the room with her if she passed! I slept with one eye open every night. We were free from most of our daily chores because we were not made to cook, clean, or do dishes; we rode that until the wheels fell off. My mother had raised us to this point to be very independent and capable of getting ourselves to school, but at my aunt's house we got rides.

Reality hit when my mother called us and told us that we had to come and get the rest of our things. It did not make sense for her to pay for a three-bedroom apartment when only two rooms were being used. She eventually moved to San Pablo. We were officially on our own; she did not send money for anything - food, clothes, nothing. I guess she felt like anyone who was brave enough to leave home at 14 and 16 years old could support themselves. She was right; my sister got a job at Lucky Stores and

I got a job in a salon in downtown Oakland as a shampoo assistant.

Although we could not fully take care of ourselves, we were capable of having our needs met because we both had money to buy our toiletries and the extra things we wanted.

I had never been into any other salon besides my grandmother's shop. I remember feeling so scared; older guys were checking me out and the older women were looking at me like "Who's this eager little girl?" At that time, there was a salon on every corner in downtown Oakland and most of the stylists networked with each other.

I was introduced to so much while working with the salon owner, Ernie. My grandmother showed me the business side of the hair business, and Ernie showed me the game. I saw so much working for Ernie; drugs, pimping, pushing, the list goes on. Although I was young I was not naive, not even little bit. I worked with Ernie on and off for five years. During this time I was struggling through school, trying to maintain a balance between work and school. It was challenging because after school I went straight to work and by the time I got off work there was no time for homework. I did it the next morning, copying my friend's work. This became an every day ritual for me until graduation.

After the second semester of my senior year, I knew right away that I was going to have to outsmart my English teacher, Ms. Clendenon; I will never forget her name. No matter how much I tried to achieve in her class, I was constantly failing tests and I felt like I had no support from her as a teacher. After a whole semester of getting nothing but D's in her class, I started looking for an adult school so that I could take English and still get credit to graduate with my class.

On Wednesdays, instead of going to work, I went to night school. Most of my friends had no idea what I was going through. I went to high school with kids whose parents were doctors, lawyers, and professional baseball and football players.

All of my school years were spent in predominantly all white schools, and I never considered myself to be pretty or cute. I thought that being pretty meant that you were mixed with white and black or whatever in order to be considered pretty. I had low self-esteem because of my skin color, weight, and hair. I did not have long flowing hair like most of my peers, and even though my mother always told me that I was beautiful, I would think that she was biased.

I had to look the part and not let my friends and peers know I had to take care of myself, so I started stealing clothes from stores like Nordstrom's and Saks Fifth Ave. Yes, I had Bentley tastes with a McDonald's budget. I got by with this way of life without getting caught for years. Our high school was a performing arts school, and I had to audition to get into Skyline. The music teacher Mr. Grout came to Montera Junior High to audition singers and that's how I got in; it was not because I lived in the district. Great people like Tom Hanks, Gary Payton, Ledisi, Diane Valentine, and a host of other successful people came out of Skyline.

My senior year finally came and it was time for all the senior activities like grad night, senior ball, and senior pictures. With my earnings, all I could afford was grad night, although I paid for my trip I was still a little short on cash. I needed a bathing suit, a casual outfit for grad night itself and miscellaneous things, so my friends and I went to the Nordstrom's Center in San Francisco and racked up. We had a swim suit for just about every day of the trip, nice poolside garments, and halters. As we were leaving, I noticed two men walking out with us with walkie talkies in their hands, and before we knew it we were in custody at Nordstrom's Loss Prevention. We were under age and they just cited us and let us go, which was a breeze to me because my grandmother didn't find out thanks to my sister; she rescued me every time. Although I got caught, I was still drawn to the adrenalin rush of getting away with something. I always looked the part, spoke the part; no one would ever guess that I was stealing. This too was a sickness, I always had money to buy the things that I wanted, but this was a sickness; I would buy something and get something free - my very own buy-one-get-one free deal for every store I went into. I continued to steal and then graduated to writing bad checks, basically closing accounts and going to rack up in the stores the same day. I did these things to survive and look good at the same time. I always believed in multiple streams of income at an early age, by any means necessary. I had no integrity at all.

I graduated from high school in June of 1991 and I immediately enrolled in beauty school. Beginning the summer of 1991, I attended Laney College, a community college in Oakland known for having a great cosmetology program. At the same time, I worked at Thrifty's; I was on track, ready for the next chapter in my life. My cousin Kim and I started a duo group called Studio II. We sang for cotillions, weddings, you name it, we were there singing our hearts out. My mother would accompany us on the piano while my younger brother Sedric was on the drums. We were what you called a family band. We later started a three girl group with our friend from school called Image. Before Destiny's Child, Escape, and SWV, Image was ready. We were vocally trained by Butch Stafford to blend together, and we had a Supremes-like sound. Unfortunately, right before we were signed to Mercury Records, there were irreconcilable differences.

I had put a lot of time into rehearsing with Image, so needless to say I was disappointed. Singing and music had always been my life as a child, along with styling hair. This situation shot my confidence way down and I felt like I would never sing again. I felt like I wasn't good enough to do it by myself until one day my mother pulled me to the side and said, "Who asked Anita Baker to leave her group? Who kicked Aretha Franklin out of her group?" I didn't have an answer. She said, "Well then, who is going to kick you out of your group?" At that moment I was instantly empowered. For the first time in my life I felt like I could be a solo lead singer, but there was still something inside of me that wanted to sing in a group. Image was recording a CD in New York and I felt like leaving Oakland too, just to save face so that no one would ask me why wasn't in New York. I decided to finish my schooling for a beauty license in North Carolina at Dudley Beauty College. I applied and was accepted, but the challenge was that I had no money to get there or pay for tuition so I continued at Laney College in Oakland where I studied hair for two years.

About a month later, I unexpectedly received a page on my

beeper from an unfamiliar number. I called the number back and it was Dangerous Music Studios. I did not know who was calling me from there because I did not yet know Too Short or anyone in his entourage. I said "Someone called Stacy?" The secretary said, "Yes, hold on." This guy comes to the phone and said, "This is Banks. I heard you were no longer in the group Image. Would you like to do some work for me?" I was floored. Boy, how news travels fast in the music industry. I swallowed and said "Yes, of course." He said, "When do you want to meet?" We met up, and Banks reminded me that we had met at the Gavin, a Bay Area convention, a year before. Well, it was history from there. I thought, "Wow! This is the guy who does all of Too Short's beats and this could something big for me." Banks was working on his first album *"Sittin' on Something Phat"*. I sang on his first single *Late Night Freak*. It was a little degrading to me because it wasn't real singing; I was just really talking nasty but I got paid and was on the payroll for years to come.

My life drastically changed after working with Banks. I was getting acknowledged by other artists, and I was finally among the recognized; I became a part of the Dangerous Music family as well as a part of Oakland's hip hop music history and Bay Area rap artists were seeking me out for vocals. Eventually I worked on projects that featured Tupac, MC Breed, Dr. Dre, Mac 10, and Spice 1. I now had multiple streams of income doing what I loved!

Ant Banks became a mentor to me, showing me the ropes of the industry and making sure I was on top of my business. I began working long hours in the studio recording two sometimes three songs in a day.

I had no idea what went on behind the scenes while working at Dangerous Music with Ant. I never just hung out at the studio; if I was there, I was working. One weekend, Ant let me borrow his truck because I was moving. After I finished moving my things, I took the truck back to the studio on Myrtle Street and right after I left, someone shot up the truck and the studio. I was devastated; I could have lost my life. Everybody in Oakland knew that the truck belonged to Ant, so they could have shot at me while driving. Thank God there was a rule in the streets back then that you didn't shoot women and children. With today's lack of those same rules, I would have been dead. This was a wake up call for me but I still did not listen, I continued to be involved in every way. Ant kept me working in the studio; Otis, Shug, and I worked a lot together on most of his projects.

By 1993 I graduated from beauty school, and my grandmother's sorority sister was retiring from her hair salon. She wanted me to take over the salon under my own name which was such a blessing to me because I finally was on my way to owning my own salon and having people work for me. I was on top of the world. I graduated in June and by January 1994, I was a salon owner. Things were looking up for me; I was grateful for everything that was coming my way. I was working with one of the hottest producers from the Bay Area and I was a salon owner. Life was grand.

Owning my business had it's ups and downs. At 21 years old I thought, "This is not bad, I am finally living my dreams." The rest of my friends were still in college or just hanging out. It was really difficult for me to buckle down and take my business seriously.

My mother would come to Oakland to help me out, taking appointments, answering phones, and doing the bookkeeping. This was a tremendous help for me because I had no knowledge of the business side of things; I just knew how to do hair and loved doing it. After my first year of business, my mother did my end of the year accounting and found that $12,000 was unaccounted for. My mother was a great businessperson and wanted me to be successful. She and my sister called a meeting to ask me what I did with the unaccounted money. I was quite upset; I felt like it was my money, who cares, and what business was it of hers to ask me? When she explained that it was considered embezzlement, she got my attention. I had only heard the word embezzlement with jail at the end of it. I had stolen twelve thousand dollars from myself. How could I do such a thing? After going through receipts, I found I had spent all of that money on clothes, partying, and going out of town on escapades.

This made me buckle down for sure. My mother sat me down and kept it real with me and told me that I needed to be at the salon at all times. She said customers did not want to talk to an answering machine, and if I had walk-ins I needed to be there. If I was gone they would go to somewhere else. I eventually got serious about my business but I still had that Oakland hustler's mentality. I always believed in multiple streams of income; how I got it didn't matter to me. It was by any means necessary and I was willing to take risks to make that happen.

Back in the 80s and 90s, the rental car companies were located on Oakland Airport property. Thanks to me, all that has changed. I began to steal cars from Alamo Rental on the side while running my business, and I rented stolen cars to people who could not get them on their own. I would tell them that they only had a limited time to drive the car before it would appear on the hot sheet. Once they said OK, the deal was sealed. Just like getting over without getting caught by the clothing stores, this too was addictive. Everybody in town came to me to get a car. This was so lucrative for me, and I kept it going for months. I had so many cars, I was giving them away. I had even gotten my little sister a car, a brand new 1993 Ford Taurus. She had it for a whole month. My father and everybody else wanted to know how Sabrina had gotten a car and wondered how was she putting gas in it when she didn't have a job. My sister rode that car until the wheels literally fell off; she did not do any maintenance on the car at all, she just drove it! After Sabrina's car died, instead of taking that as a sign from God to stop doing what I was doing, I got her another car. I was low on cash and this time we were not renting, we were going to take this next car to the chop shop. We went to Alamo at the airport and this time the rental agreement didn't work. We had a Chevy Lumina that was stolen and rode that car to get another car. How dumb were we? We drove into the rental lot with the stolen car, and my cousin Mary hopped out and got into a Lexus, fully loaded with leather seats. As we pulled up to the gate, the security guard would not let the Lexus through. He told us to take it back, that it was not in the computer as a rented vehicle. Instead of her taking the car back, she busted through the gates, breaking them down as we sped off! We pulled over to let my sister and her boyfriend take the car so that we could put it up at the chop shop before the police could find it. Mary and I were in the other stolen car and told them to go straight to the garage.

Instead of going to the garage, they decided to joy ride through East Oakland. The car was on the hot sheet the moment we drove off, and OPD spotted the stolen car and immediately pursued her in a chase. My sister was driving and gave the police an O.J Simpson-style chase, doing the speed limit but not stopping. Before they knew it, the officer called for backup. Later I found out the officer was a high school friend of mine. He and I were good friends; we went to junior high school together too. With a last name like Hogg, he knew my sister had to be my relative; there just were not a lot of Hoggs in Oakland. By the time she finally stopped, the whole force was on her. When he saw her ID, he asked her "Are you Stacy Hogg's sister?" She said, "Yes." He explained to her they would not have had to call for backup and go through all of that if she just would have pulled over; now he couldn't do anything. My sister went to jail and that's when "Operation Rentals" was over. I felt so bad because I had to explain to my family why she was in jail. We came up with the world's biggest lie so no one ever knew I had anything to do with it. I visited her in jail and I put money on her books, and told her that she had to ride with the lie for not following the script. It still did not stop me, though; I was just doing it because I was getting away with it. Addiction! I was addicted to stealing cars and making fast money, all while still running my hair establishment. Nobody ever knew. The last and final straw was when we went back and I got a fully loaded 1995 Cadillac; this car was not on the hot sheet. I had been driving the car in the hood of West Oakland right past the police for about a week. One day, my then boyfriend was running the block and heard that the car I was driving was stolen and he asked me to move it off the block. David and I were not on good terms, so me being me, I told him that the car was not stolen and I wasn't moving it! In my mind, it was not stolen. David did not like that and he had all the youngsters in the hood jack the car. They stripped it from head to toe causing more attention to be drawn to it. They took the battery, the seats, the emblems, tires, everything. I calmly went to the car and got all of my things out.

Shortly after that, the car was hot. The police found out that the car was stolen, remembered seeing me drive it through the hood, and immediately came to my salon to question me. I rolled with the old lie that it was my friend's car and I did not know that it was stolen. They immediately arrested me on the spot and I kept to my story. I played the victim role, and since I knew members of the task force and a host of police officers, I was able to name drop and get off on the spot. Ironically everyone who stripped the car went to jail. I watched all of those people go to jail for a car I stole. I gave up; stealing cars was not for me. I closed that chapter of my life for good. Even though I made fast money, it wasn't worth it at the end of the day. I was not put on this earth to be a car broker, and a stolen car broker at that.

All the dirt that I had gotten away with finally caught up to me. I wrote my last bad check in a major department store, and was arrested and taken to Santa Rita Jail in Alameda County. I was so scared; I had never even seen the inside of a jail except to visit my sister. My most extreme experience up to that point was being put in the back of a police car. When they booked me, I was placed in a pod with women who didn't look like women, except for maybe three of us. I've always had a bubbly personality and it wasn't hard to converse, but I knew right away that this was definitely not the right place for me. I was there for seven days and I learned quickly how things operated in jail. I went to the deputy and told her I was a licensed stylist; she allowed me to get the clippers and liners out of the hair box they kept in a locked room. I started cutting hair for all the women that wanted to look like men. I was trading hair cuts for toiletries and extra snacks. I called my sister Sherron and she asked if I needed money on my books; I laughed hysterically and told her no, I had everything I needed and more.

During my time there, a few of the inmates would tell others I had a voice, and they would ask me to sing. One night they asked the deputy to let me sing, and I was let out of my cell to do just that. I couldn't believe it! It was 10pm, way past our lock down hour, and I worried about what song I would sing. I immediately started with *Reminisce* by Mary J. Blige, and I sang my heart out.

When I was done, the deputy walked up to me and told me in a very stern voice, "I better not see you in here again! You are too talented to be locked up." I looked at her in shame. I was released a few days later, and I never looked back. I started singing more and performed in showcases.

Between stealing cars and making people look good, I somehow managed to stay in the studio. I had done four albums with Ant Banks, and after a while he started referring me to other artists. I did vocals for Spice 1, Mac 10, Bad Influence, The Click, and Mr. Ill. I worked with a group called To Be Continued, an East-West Atlantic recording artist from the Bay produced by Foster & McElroy, the producers of En Vogue. That led me to eventually work on Regina Bell's *Reaching Back* album in 1996, also produced by Foster & McElroy. My mother was proud of me; she had no idea what I was doing outside the salon and the studio, all she knew was that her daughter was working with all these artists and was running her own business.

In 1997, I sang in a talent show my cousin Kim put on at Geoffrey's Inner Circle in Oakland and she hired J-Murray, a San Francisco Bay Area comedian, to host it. I thought he was funny and cute, and after the show I approached him and told him how funny I thought he was. That wasn't the last of him; he ended up becoming my daughter's father. We had been dating for two years when I found out that I was pregnant, and that very same month we also found out that my mother had breast cancer. It was a bitter sweet situation; I was happy and sad. Here I was becoming a mother and losing my mother at the same time. I did not know if I was coming or going. My mother had her mastectomy and the cancer went into remission for a year, and when it came back it came back with a vengeance. I thought God had turned his back on me for all the dirt that I had done in the years before, for not being an obedient child, running way, you name it. My world was seemingly crashing in on me like a bad accident. My mother could not afford her apartment anymore because most of her money was going towards staying alive. Her co-pay for chemotherapy was $800, and her husband had left her for another woman. She was really struggling due to the fact that she could not work and had to get chemotherapy. The neighborhood that she moved to was not safe so I moved in with her for a little while, and a little while was all it was; I immediately started looking for a place to stay outside of Oakland. When my place was ready, I moved her in with me and I was glad because I could not take my mother living in that kind of environment. The area I moved to was quiet and she could rest. My mother was very supportive even though she was not very pleased that I was going to be a single parent. I didn't want to get married just because I was pregnant; that's what my grandparents made her do, but I was grown and capable of making my own choices and I chose to do it alone. My mother ended up being a single parent but she never married my father with the intentions of leaving him or raising my sister and I alone. For me to go into the journey of parenthood with no commitment was ludicrous to her.

During the first months of my pregnancy, I was getting a lot of calls to do background vocal work. I had just worked with Regina Belle on her *Reaching Back* album, and Ricky Waters from the San Francisco 49ers heard about me and called me to do some background vocals on his music project. I was about three months pregnant and was still going through the nausea stage. When I got to his house, I could not believe I was at Ricky Waters' house about to record with him. We started listening to the music that I was going to sing and record to and once it was time for me to go into the vocal booth, I started throwing up and had to ask to be excused from the session. I finally got it together and came back, knocking the session out in an hour or two. After I left the session, I was worried about how I was going to be pregnant and pull the long hours at the studio *and* the salon. I was going to have to give up something and that something was going to have to be my music so that I could be present for my baby. Time passed and my due date could not come fast enough; I stayed at my sister's house in Oakland so that I was closer to the hospital. My due date was December 3rd which was my sister Sherron's birthday, but Ms. Jaelyn did not come until the 9th, which was the same birthday as my cousins, Alicia and Kim.

My labor went well; I was in labor for six hours and with the help of an epidural it made pushing so much easier. I didn't know any differently. My daughter's father was there with the video camera throughout all of my labor and birth, and we were able to capture her birth. I just wanted to get this baby out of me so that I could start my new life with her. Jaelyn was 9 pounds 3 ounces. I tell people all the time she came out like a toddler, I never had an infant. She was so cute! She had a round face and she looked just like her daddy. I remember being so happy but in the back of my mind I was so worried about my mother. I needed her now more than ever.

It hurt my heart that three months after Jaelyn was born the cancer had came back so forcefully that my mother could not even hold my baby on her own; I had to sit with her and help her. The fact that she could not hold my baby and do other simple things tore me up. After about three months, my daughter's father finally came clean and told me he and another woman were an item, and asked that I respect that.

We went to court for custody and the outcome was that he would have her Thursday through Sunday, and she would be with me Sunday night to Thursday. I almost lost my mind because he was playing this game so that he would not have to pay child support. Jaelyn was never with him; his girlfriend had my baby every weekend while he was out chasing me at the clubs I was singing at or at the clubs I would frequent on the weekends. I went through anxiety attacks because I could not reach anyone to check on my daughter. She was just five months old; I almost lost my mind. Jason was gone all the time and the only number I had was his cell phone so when I called to check on my daughter he never knew where or how she was. She was always with the new girlfriend.

Six months later, I was pulled over for a routine traffic stop and discovered I had a no-bail warrant for my arrest for non-payment of the restitution for a DUI I had gotten a while back. Although I had completed the classes, I still had not paid the fines and ended right back in Santa Rita, this time for thirty days. All I could think about was that I didn't want to see the deputy that had told me she didn't want to see me back there. I was no stranger to life behind bars, but this time I had a baby. I kept thinking about

36

my mother telling me she didn't know what kind of mother I was going to be, that my baby needed me, and to stay on top of my business. I couldn't be there for my child, and that scared me straight! It was no longer just me, I had a new little life that was depending on me. On top of all that, I had a show coming up at Mingles, where I sang on Fridays. I called my music director BJ collect and told him not to cancel our gig. He thought I was absolutely crazy!

God was truly on my side. I was released early, after having served only two weeks and was able to make it to my gig. I was so glad that all worked out in my favor.

About a year later, my mother's cancer had moved from her breast to her vital organs; it wasn't looking too good and the doctors had given her six months to live. I was so afraid! One Saturday, Jason called and said that my baby had a seizure. I thought, "Oh my God, my mother's dying and now I find out that my baby has seizures?" I was on the highway from West Oakland to Richmond, and fast. When I arrived, Jason was there with his mother and girlfriend, and she and I were not on the best of terms; there was so much tension between her and I. I asked the doctor to excuse her from the room so that I could relax. The doctor asked her to leave and I began to ask all the necessary questions. The doctors told me that Jaelyn was not epileptic, the seizure was caused by a fever. They told me she would have febrile seizures until she was four year old. I was so happy because eventually she would grow out of it, and I would not have to deal with it after age four; that was a blessing. However, in the back of my mind it was still something I feared would return.

I thought Jason's girlfriend had left, but this woman sat outside in her car until we were finished so that she could fight me. We were walking out of the hospital and out of nowhere she jumped out at me and challenged me to a fight. I jumped into my car and told her to get in front of the car because I was going to finish her for good; she would no longer harass me and bother me. Luckily, the police station was right across the street from the hospital. I tried to run her over with my car and missed her, and finally I drove to the police station and made a police report.

Dealing with all of this drama as well as losing my mother was too much for one person, but through it all I told myself that God was not going to put more on me than I could bear. I began to seek ways to ease my pain by taking ecstasy pills. I was on ecstasy pretty heavily, popping two pills at a time. My weight began to come down drastically; you could see my collar bone because I was so skinny. My mind was in chaos. I had no peace whatsoever. I was constantly fighting with my daughter's father, his girlfriend, and his mother. This continued until my mother died. If I did not have my mother through all of this, I would have been a complete wreck.

My mother helped me through a lot. I didn't want to burden her with my problems, but she knew I was going through it. I remember one day she asked me if I was snorting cocaine. I weighed 100 pounds and I had a bobble head, my body was small and my face was still fat. That's a sure way to tell that someone is not losing weight correctly. Every day I would pick my mother's brain about little things, tell her I was sorry for being such a bad kid, and tell her how much I appreciated all that she had done for me. During this time I thought it would be smart to try and heal my relationship with my father so I spent a lot of time observing him and his family. I needed to know why my father never gave me hugs or told me he loved me. What I found is that on his side of the family there was no affection; no one kissed, hugged, or greeted each other, and for some reason this stood out to me in huge way. For the first time I noticed that they shared no affection. This made me realize that the way my father was treating me and my sisters was the only way he knew how to treat us because that was how he was raised. For the first time in my life I felt sorry for my dad; his parents gave him material things in place of love and now to this day my grandmother feels guilty for it, and trust me he fuels that guilt by putting more blame on her every chance he gets.

It was getting closer to the fifth month out of six of my mother's life expectancy, and all this time I had been praying for God to heal her. The more I prayed for God to heal her, the more the cancer spread. I got really scared; am I killing my mother by praying for this? Well, no. God was answering my prayers. Her ultimate healing was to remove her spirit from that sick body. Trust me, I didn't understand that at the time, it came to me after she was gone. I was not dealing with the fact that my mother was about to leave this earth.

Four weeks before she died my mother, sister, and I went to pick out her casket. That was most dreary day of my life; I could not believe that I was actually going to the casket shop, and with her. How did she feel, what was going on in her mind? I could never imagine. We were listening to Eric Benet's song "All We Are is Dust in the Wind". I held back my tears; I did not want my mother to see me cry. When we got there my mother looked at me and my sister and said, "OK girls, which one is it going to be? This is my final bed so it's got to be nice." My sister and I just looked at each other in dismay. We went straight to a very nice white and gold casket. We all decided on this particular casket and then my mother pulled her credit card out to put the deposit on the casket. I couldn't take it; I can't even begin to tell you what was going through my mind. My mother was so courageous through this whole ordeal, from day one. When she had her breast removed she answered her hospital phone, "One Titty Kitty's Room." My mother was hilarious! She would put her fake breast on her bald head and call herself Grandmother Unit, so whenever our children would get into trouble or cry she would put the fake breast on her head and say "Grandmother Unit to the rescue!" and would come running out of her room with this plastic breast on her head. Mother kept this experience fun and adventurous.

When we got back from the casket warehouse she began to write her obituary. This was also too much for me, but I saw her strength and I had to finally face reality; no ecstasy could cloud this day at all. This was it. I had to face my fear of being without my mother. I knew that the time was near. I had to come to grips that one day soon my mother was going to be leaving me.

That next day my mother's good friend Hershel came by. Hershel used to be a part of Grand Central Station with Larry Gram and was also a Jehovah's Witness. I asked him to play Misty for me because my mother could no longer sit up to play the piano. He got half way through the song and she began to cry. The tears rolled down my face too because this was my connection to my mother. I was her music child and to know that my band members and my mother were leaving me was so hurtful. What was I going to do? At that time I felt that I had emotionally neglected my daughter because all, and I mean all, of my attention went to my mother. I felt pulled in two directions; my mother needed me and so did my new baby but I was so spiritually empty that I was no good to either of them. I knew the day that I had always feared was near.

I had a shop full of clients. I had been working all day, and my brother had just flown in from South Carolina. When he got there he went upstairs to where my mother was and started singing all of the songs she sang to him when he was a child. We all had songs. I remember her moaning to let him know that she knew he was there; it was a trip because she had not been responding. We knew that this was the end. I felt so helpless; this was it. Down to the wire. My mother finally passed the next morning on June 16th, 2000. It was a mixed feeling for me; on one side I felt relief and on the other side I felt hurt that she was gone. My mother was gone without my permission. I didn't want her to go but God had the last say and I had to come to terms with that. My sister and I just looked at each other and said, "We did it." We felt like we had walked her to the other side but we could not cross over with her.

I immediately got into her hospital bed in the living room, and I laid with her body until the mortuary came. I felt like I wanted to be with her until she turned cold because as long as there was heat, there was some life there. By the time the coroner came, her body had gotten cold and I told them to take her. She was with me in spirit, the body was then only a shell.

After that I went downstairs to my clients and serviced each and every one of them with a smile. I knew my mother would be so proud of me for handling my business that way. Most of my clients were telling me how sorry they were but I didn't want anyone to feel sorry for me. I wanted to finish their hair and go home. I wanted to be alone with my sister and brother because we all felt the same way. I wanted to reminisce and think of the good days, but all that kept going through my mind were the last days of her suffering; I had mixed emotions. I was happy, I was lonely, I was sad, I was mad...I didn't know exactly how or what to feel.

No matter how much you prepare yourself for a loved one's death, regardless of how old they are, you never are fully prepared for that day, and although I felt like we took it well, I was still in shock that my mommy was gone.

My mother asked me to promise her that I would make sure her head was not going to be shown because of the burn from the radiation treatments, so I went out with my sister and we found an African store. We bought her a 14 carat gold silk African made dress and head wrap for her to be buried in.

Three days later it was time for me to go to the mortuary to do my mothers make-up and wrap up her head. My sister made me go with my aunt which was a disaster because all my aunt did from the time we got there until we left was screamed and hollered "My sister!" Before I was done I had to ask my aunt to leave. I explained to her that while I knew it was her sister that had passed and I understood that she had known her longer, I was trying to provide a service to my mother and hold myself up at the same time. She was supposed to be support for me and I had to hold her up? It was hilarious.

I finished her make-up and her wrap that matched her gown. If I may say so, I did an excellent job. Thanks MAC! I surprised myself, she looked amazing. I could not believe that I had just worked on a dead body and my mother's at that. The Bible's words are true; love does conquer all fear.

After the services, we invited all of her musician friends including her husband over to the house for food and a jam session. We ordered a table and chairs for the backyard and jammed the night away. We would have it no other way, singing and jamming is what she would have been doing if she was here. We had so much support before the funeral from family, but it's funny how everyone called to see how we were doing before the funeral but as soon as the funeral was over everyone just disappeared.

My birthday was two months later, and every year my

mother would have "the birthday talk" with me as an evaluation of where I've been and what my future goals were. This was the first year without her and my birthday talk, and it was my worst. I cried like a little baby crying for milk. I screamed MAMA! so loud I hoped that she would hear me and just appear out of nowhere and hug me.

That night I went to a well known Mexican hole in the wall called Mexi-Cali Rose and ordered three Cadillac margaritas. Their drinks aren't watered down, if you know what I mean. When I got ready to leave I saw three of everything. I knew that I was drunk, but in my mind I could make it home, and I tried. The next thing I knew I was behind the wheel and off I went. As I was driving I felt myself swerving but I kept saying to myself, "You can make it". After about a mile or so I saw flashing lights and surrendered myself to the police. I got what you call a "friendly DUI". I call it that because I was well over the 0.8 limit; as a matter of fact I was a candidate to go to jail and sober up. I can't tell you what I said to them, but the next thing I knew I was at the jail and they let me call a friend to pick me up. They didn't tow my car; they told my friend where they parked it so that I could go get it the next day! Talk about being in God's favor.

I eventually had to go to DUI school and pay a ton of fines. When I gave the lady my first and last name she asked me if I knew a Morris Hogg. I said, "Yes, that's my father." I was so embarrassed that my father's name was in a data file for attending the same class. I too had the same chemical imbalance that he had when it came to alcohol, and here I was following in his footsteps with a DUI history. After that, it made me want to get help for myself because I wanted to stop the curse that was passed down to me. After two years, I was through with all the madness and ready for change. I needed to be who my mother raised me to be and spread my wings.

III
Imagine

After my mother died in 2000, God was showing me all the signs that it was time for me to leave Oakland. I ignored Him for two years, continuing to drink myself into toxic comas. Nothing was working in my life, I was a wreck. God wanted me to start on a new path, and it was the purpose leading up to my new journey in life. In my mind I was moving to Arizona. I had the Phoenix newspaper sent to my salon, I had a friend that did real estate who was to show me around; I thought I was on my way. But when things were not working out the way I planned, I asked God, "OK, what is it? I know you don't want me to stay here in Oakland. Where do you want me to go?" He said, "Los Angeles." and I flat out said, "No!" I did not fully understand what God was saying. I thought I knew my own way and the Bible says a man's steps are directed by the Lord. (Proverbs 20:20:20) How then do I know my own way? My daughter's father had just moved to Southern California with his new girlfriend and I was worried about what people would say. I felt like people were going to think that I moved there because he did.

After about six months, I surrendered and said, "OK, God, I'll try LA." My business had begun to plunge and I had nothing to lose anyway. I still felt like LA didn't need me. Everybody there was either a singer, actress, or bartender. I would be like a diamond in the rough.

I began to look for jobs on movie sound stages at the WB, Disney, and host of other places doing hair jobs, but to get hired in the film and television industry you have to work for free on a SAG (Screen Actors Guild) show or movie, or apply for SAG and hope to get a job. I applied but nothing happened, so I kept trying other avenues but I didn't stop there. I went another route; the TV sets had not seen the last of me.

I went to the web site for Hair Club for Men. I saw that they needed a hair technician for their Glendale office in

California. Hair loss was not exactly what I was looking for, but I figured what the heck, it's a job. I might get a chance to learn something new and advance myself in hair, and I didn't have to work in a salon which would have been devastating to me since I had owned my own business for 6 years. I didn't feel like I could go back to paying booth rent in someone else's hair salon.

I filled out an online application and to my surprise they called me back the next day. Now for me this was big because I had never worked for a corporation as large as this, and it was pertaining to hair knowledge on a whole other level in the hair industry. I ended up getting a second phone interview which was a little intense because they wanted me to assure them that I had no intentions of opening my own salon again. They were reluctant to hire me, but when I went into the formal interview my boss was a black woman named Vanice. Vanice and I looked at each other and just started cracking up because we both were speaking on the phone with our professional voices on the phone interviews, and neither one of us knew that the other was black. So needless to say we clicked and I was hired. Now it just so happened that the day I was hired, the consultant that was there at the time quit as she was getting married and was moving. Vanice was desperate for a consultant and during my interview she asked me if I knew anything about sales or consulting. Now let this be a lesson: never turn down a job as long as you have eyes, your hearing, and a brain. You can always learn, and that's what I did. I quickly said yes and she said, "Then you have the job, all I need from you is a resume." That's it? I went right home and made a resume that said I had been in sales for five years which was not totally a lie but somewhat of an exaggeration.

I got the job the next day and began training for two weeks. They sent me to New Orleans for a week and then to Cleveland, Ohio for a week. By the time I got back from training, my boss had already found me a place to live; it felt like God was really showing out this time, like everything started coming into place without me even lifting a finger. Somehow that was the universe's way of letting me know that I was right where I was supposed to be. When things happen in your life that just flow like running

44

water, roll with it. It is or it isn't, it's the truth by the way it feels.

Because of the fact that I was originally hired as a stylist, they wrote in my contract that if my sales went below fifty percent they would not fire me, they would just automatically move me into a stylist position since that was the position I originally applied for. Nine months into my job that is exactly what happened; my boss went to a corporate manger's conference in Las Vegas and the new owners of the company made some comments about taking the black women off of the infomercial but they could not afford to train the stylist on how to do black hair. Additionally, there were not enough black women coming into the company because they could not afford it. Vanice called the Glendale office from her hotel room in tears; she could not believe what she had heard. For me it was a letdown because people had gotten word that there was a black consultant in Glendale and I was seeing at least five black men and women a week, which was a dramatic change from when I had started working for them. When Vanice came back, she quit the next week; she could not take it and I couldn't blame her. I felt like I wanted to leave too but I couldn't walk away from a job without another one to replace it. I was also in an unfamiliar place with no safety nets; it just wasn't possible for me to quit. I hung in there as a consultant for as long as I could.

Anyone who has ever been in sales knows that if you believe in the product you're selling you will do well. The problem was not that I did not believe in the product, but that I had lost faith in the company as a whole. I figured if they did not want to pay extra money to train stylists on ethnic hair then why would I bring blacks into the company? My sales plunged after that; they sent me to training again and everything. Nothing worked. One thing that I knew from being in business for myself in the hair industry is that black women will spend some money on their hair!

I had dope fiends and crack heads in Oakland pay me for their hair two weeks in advance so that they would not smoke the money up. Whoever told these business men that black women couldn't afford the hair was not talking to the right people. When the company found out that Vanice left because of what she heard in the meeting, they rethought their decision and kept the African

American lady in the infomercial. I finally got a new boss and was starting my training as a stylist. I was in training for about three weeks, and then they sent me out to the wolves. I became what you called an NBI stylist. That means that I was the stylist that did the replacement procedure the first time they came into the company. This was good for me because of my background and I was doing what I truly loved doing - making people look good. This was like heaven to me. The stylist that I worked with was cool about showing me the ropes because I had to learn quickly and efficiently. In my four years with the company I learned a lot, and I was so excited about learning something new and being good at it. Working in corporate America was new to me but I realized quickly that I didn't fit in. Two years passed and I just could not take the corporate America environment anymore; my heart was too big. In corporate America it's all about business without heart. They were not kid friendly, and there would be times that I had no babysitter on weekends and they made it mandatory that I work weekends. I had Armenian co-workers that were not too friendly and I got to a place where I did not want to go into the office anymore. I knew I would be on my way out fast; family comes first.

***

October 20ᵗʰ 2004. My manager at Hair Club called me in to the office and told me that I was going to have to resign if I couldn't work on Saturdays. I thought, "What bullshit! I have to quit my job because I don't have a sitter on Saturdays?" I told them that I was not quitting my job; I loved the work that I did. There were only two options: quit or be fired; I chose to be fired. I was so scared; I didn't know where my next meal was going to come from, let alone how we were going meet our bills. To my surprise, a handful of clients left the company and came with me; this was a blessing. I had clients on the side that were keeping me afloat. Ironically, my cousin had gotten a singing gig all the way in Japan and wanted me to go with her for three months. That sounded good and I had always dreamed of going to Japan. I began to think about going out there just to hang out but it didn't make sense financially because I still needed a place to come home to at the end of the day and I had to feed my daughter. I called Brenda Vaughn, the agent working with us, and I asked her if she could book me a gig as well. I did not care if it was just doing hair or tap dancing, I needed to make money for the three months that I was there. This trip was going to be the epitome of walking by faith and in the night by sight. Brenda hooked me up with Hirano, a Japanese agent. He did not have a concrete gig for me but he told me to come and he would see what he could do. Kim paid for my ticket under the agreement that if I got a gig I would pay her back. I had a very short time to get my passport and get my business straight. I had to find a non-surgical facility for my clients for the three months that I would be gone and get my daughter situated with her father. I did all of this in two weeks.

***

September 7, 2004. It was Labor Day weekend and my birthday. We went home to Oakland because we were leaving out of San Francisco Airport, and at this time of the year my family always has a family reunion so my daughter and I went to the BBQ the day before. I was having fun up until it was time for me to leave my baby; that was one of the hardest things for me to do besides telling my mother it was OK to take her final resting place when she passed. I got an anxiety attack at the last minute and broke down crying. Although I was leaving her with her father and grandmother, I had never been that far away from her, and I was so afraid to go to Japan not knowing if I was going to get a job singing. I finally pulled it together and said my goodbyes, and the next day we were on our way to Narita Airport in Japan. We left out of San Francisco Airport at about 8:00am. My father brought me, and Auntie Carolyn and Uncle Carl brought Kim. You should have seen us; we looked like we were never coming back. You know us; we over pack on three day trips and we were going to be gone for three months, so you know how we looked. Both of our bags were overweight so we had to pay an additional fee. Before getting on the plane, I led us in prayer and as I prayed tears rolled down all of our faces. It was an emotional moment, especially for me because I did not know what I was going to do if I didn't get a job while being there for three months. Our flight was twelve hours long and it was a pretty good flight; no turbulence, a smooth ride. The only problem we had was this little dog that kept barking; we nicknamed him Arf-Arf. It was so funny! When we got to Japan, it was like being lost in translation for real, nobody spoke a lick of English and in Japan, you are in their country so they expect for you to know their language. They are not trying to stick around to try to understand what you're trying to say. If you don't have a translator you must get a book on how to communicate. If not, tough luck!

We took a shuttle from the airport into Tokyo to meet the Japanese agent, Hirano, who immediately put me on the Shinkansen (high speed railway) to Nagoya; he had a gig for me at Club Voice which was a "live house". I was so amazed because I actually had a gig that quickly! I was not in Japan two hours and had already gotten work. I was so afraid to get on the Shinkansen train by myself because here I was in a foreign country traveling five hundred miles south, by myself. Kim and I just looked at each other and said this is it; this is what we came here for. As the train pulled off, we were still looking at each other like Netty and Celie from the movie, *The Color Purple*.

When I arrived in Nagoya, the club owner was at the train station to pick me up and get me settled. She was a brunette and tall for a Japanese woman. She had an exotic look and was high fashioned. I was so surprised because her English was great and she seemed really down to earth. Later on I found out why she was so down to earth. She was married to the black band director, Bruce, who played in the club.

She then took me to what they called my 'mansion' in the heart of Nagoya; to me it was far from a mansion because the outside looked like the high rises on Good Times. The inside was so small that only one person could fit. It was a jail cell with a kitchen, but I did not complain. I was in Japan!

I only had one hour to get my things settled in and then was off to the club for rehearsal. When we arrived at the club the band was already there; they were all in their late 30's to mid 40's. The drummer, Allan, the other lead vocalist, Bill, and Kit the bass player were all cold pieces of work. They all had their own set of issues, but who doesn't?

We went over a couple of songs for that night and it was on and poppin'. Each night we had to wear something different and the first night was black so it wasn't very difficult for me to hook up an outfit. I did my make-up and hair, and was ready for the night.

My first night was really challenging because I had to sing while people blew cigarette smoke into my face. That was the most challenging thing I had to go through. I remember singing and wanting to choke at the same time; it was hilarious. I didn't care though, all I could think about was that I was in Japan and who cares if I die of smoke inhalation, at least I would die doing what I loved to do.

After about a week I got used to the cigarette smoke and during the long breaks in between each set I would go across the street to the internet cafe to email Kim in Tokyo and to talk to family and friends back home in the US. I was beginning to miss my daughter Jaelyn; it had finally set in that if anything happened to her I could not just get to her like I would have wanted to. I had anxiety attacks and called my sister to tell her to check on her. Although she was with her grandmother and her dad, I still felt uneasy about being that far without my baby. I wrote her letters and called at least twice a week. My agent bought me a cell phone but even that came with a price. My phone bill was deducted from my pay at the end of the month so I really had to monitor my calls, especially to the US.

I finally began to use my time to soul search and look at myself in the mirror for some introspection. Surprisingly, I didn't like what I saw. I began to try to meditate and look deep within my spirit. It was in Japan that I felt like I was so close to my mother. It was in Japan that I said I would start a cancer foundation in my mother's memory. I wanted to give back. One of my main programs would be a non-surgical hair replacement program using what I learned to help people. It was clear as day. God said, "What is it that you want to do?" I responded, "Help people with my talents and the gifts you have given me." I was inspired to the fullest.

My mother always told my sister and me that if she could afford it, she would have moved us to Japan to live so I felt that by me getting the rare opportunity to go to a place where my mother spent time sharing her gift was a blessing for me. I felt really close to her, and I got a chance to see what she saw. It was awesome.

The other lead singer, Bill, and I had gotten close. He was like a guardian angel and he showed me the ropes. Bill had been singing in Japan for years. He would always knock on my door to let me know our taxi driver was there to pick us up, basically keeping me on point because I was still on U.S. time. Bill was the only person that I gelled with out of our whole band because he was a warm spirit and real. He wasn't pretentious like the other guys. We would have great conversations on real life situations; we could relate in more ways than one.

Four weeks had gone by and Kim had two days off so she caught a Shinkansen to Nagoya to hear me one weekend. We had a ball. I missed her and she missed me; we were two peas in a pod. Finally after all that time just emailing, we got a chance to see each other. The next day we went shopping and sightseeing. All too quickly it was time for her to go back to Yokohama.

When Kim left, I assured her that on my off day I would come to Yokohama to spend time with her. The next week came and I was off to Yokohama to spend time with Kim at her gig.

Ironically, when I got there the musician that played for Kim at Club Dolphin had to take the day off, and our agent Hirano was looking for someone to fill in for him. I told Kim I would fill in. The thought was hilarious because I couldn't play the piano even if I tried. We thought about it and I asked what he was paying the fill-in. Hirano said it was 20,000 Yin. I told Kim to tell him yes, I would do it!

The musicians played with what they call a mini disk anyway so no one would really know if I was playing or not. This was so funny to us because we knew that I was going to fake it. We went to the mall and bought matching outfits and became

50

Studio Two again. Only this time Kim was singing and I was on the piano. Talk about hustle - we pulled that gig off well. Surprisingly, nobody knew that I was faking it; that night was a hit! About two months later it was time for us to head back to the States, our three month run had come to an end and I was ready to be back home. I missed my daughter and was a little home sick at the same time. We flew back into SFO and then took a domestic flight into LAX.

The whole time that I was on the plane coming home I was meditating on starting the foundation in my mother's memory and how I was going to use my hair replacement and musical talents to bring awareness to breast cancer. My thoughts were on how I could combine the hair and music in our programs, and it came to me. I could give cancer patients hair replacements instead of wigs; it was a hot idea and I was motivated.

Once I landed, I went straight to see my daughter; she was so happy to see me she cried! I did too. When we finally got settled at home, she and I climbed into bed and we snuggled. We talked about my trip, and I showed her pictures and gave her all of the souvenirs that I didn't send to her during my stay.

I began to take spiritual classes. I joined the Faithful Central Bible Church in LA and began to work on my mind, body, and spirit. I hired a personal trainer and began to meditate and zero in on me. Sometimes when you look in the mirror you may not like what you see; it is the first step to recovery.

I began to love myself by treating myself to the spa twice a week, getting facials, body scrubs, you name it. A good friend introduced me to a DVD "The Secret" and that DVD literally changed my life. For some reason everything I had learned in church made sense. It was like newly found knowledge that wasn't new, all of the principles were everything I knew but had never applied to my own life. Forgiveness, love thy neighbor, all of it.

When I came back to LA, I joined the AJ Zone and lost 40lbs. I maintained my healthy lifestyle with my personal trainer, Andre Riley. That next year I was invited to Usher's fundraiser for kids in New York, where I met a wonderful lady, Joy Graham, who was one of the coordinators for his event. My sister and I eventually hired her as a consultant to start our non-profit cancer foundation. Six months later, we were incorporated. I taught awareness and prevention to little girls, ages 7 and up in the Glendale after-school programs. I also bought a new car; things were really looking up for me. I began to feel better as I pulled myself up by the bootstraps.

2004. My younger brother Sedric was released from prison after serving three years for possession of narcotics with the intent to sell. They were about to release my brother right back to the same neighborhood where they had arrested him. I was outraged and challenged the California State Parole Board to release him to me in LA County. They gave me a fight, calling me a "motivational speaker". I expressed to them that I was not going out without a fight. I had to be an advocate for my brother or else they would have released him back into the same foolishness he was locked up for. He needed to get out of the rat race that he was in while living in Oakland. The parole board finally agreed to move his parole to LA County. I personally went to the top supervisor and thanked him for allowing my brother a second chance to get his life on the right track. I was so happy to have my brother with me. I had been grieving my mother alone, and now my brother was with me. I stepped out on faith, and I bought my first piece of property. I felt like I was in alignment with the universe. It's amazing what you can do if you're in the right space and there is balance in your life.

2005. I had friends in the music industry who were what you would call "working musicians"; they were always in and out of town from touring and I was always invited to the industry parties. At these parties pretty much everything was offered, from alcohol to any drug of choice. A few times I passed on it, saying 'no, thank you' all night. I continued going to the parties and hung around celebs that indulged in drugs. Once, I was at a party and the coke plate was being passed around; I decided I'd try cocaine. That was the biggest mistake of my life! It started out only on weekends and then eventually I continued to indulge to the point where I was seeking it daily. It was like I couldn't function without it.

Everything was moving so fast and I couldn't stop it. I began to snort cocaine regularly and eventually that lead to smoking it. I often asked myself how I could get caught up in this life, given that I had seen what it does to people while growing up.

Why did I wait until I was 30 years old to get hooked on drugs? I'll tell you. The devil is tricky; he came to rob, steal, and destroy. He made doing drugs with celebrities seem like a sense of higher standards, when really it was not. Each day I prayed for God to take the taste for it from me. I was high one night and got on my knees and just surrendered myself to God. The more I said no to drugs the more drugs would get handed to me on a platter! It was like the devil would tell people to give it to me, when I didn't even have money to buy it. I never understood how that happened. My faith was being tested like no other. I would be clean for a week and then back at it again; my body was going through these little withdrawals after just seven days.

I never let go of God's hand while going through all of this. I would be getting high and talking about the goodness of God. Most of the people I was getting high with were highly irritated that I wanted to talk about God and get high. I figured God was omnipotent, and He knew what I was doing. I included Him because He was still with me, even when I was getting high. (Matthew 28:20) I held on to His word!

I eventually started smoking alone, isolating myself in my walk–in closet. The guilt and shame consumed me! I lost my smile, and I looked down 80% of the time. I was unhappy and I lost love for myself. I remained functional enough to volunteer at my daughter's school, and somehow I kept her acting and gymnastic classes paid for. Two years had passed and I was on a downward spiral, and I didn't even recognize it. I was tired and my business was slowing down from not being on top of my day to day tasks. I was staying up all night and sleeping all day. I made good money but not enough to take weeks off at a time. Every time I got high I would call my sister. She would say, "Stacy, you keep repeating yourself. What's wrong with you?" I would tell her, "I don't want you to forget what I said." It was like I was secretly reaching out for help from her but I could not bring myself to tell her what I was really doing.

All is well...

Today is a good day
Everything is working out for my life
I love and approve of myself
Everything is working out for my highest good.

Whatever I need comes to me
I trust the process of life to bring me every thing I need.
Everything is working in divine order.

Stacy, you are wonderful and I love you.
Today is the best day of my life.
Everything I need to know is revealed to me.

All is well

I have a perfect living space and
I now create a wonderful foundation for my life
For my business and my surroundings.
I deserve the best, and I accept it now.

All is well.....

All is well.....

Thank God, all is well!!!

IV
Changes

June 13th,2007. I got a call from my sister. She said that my grandmother only had twenty-four hours to live. Although my grandmother had been suffering from Alzheimer's for about fifteen years, it was still a reality check to me that she was leaving us. I was not ready for this; my mind was in shambles because of the chemical imbalance from drugs and I didn't want to face the reality of having to bury my grandmother. I quickly called my brother and told him the news. He immediately told me to come and get him. Now this was a test of my faith; I had little to no money to travel home and my brother was newly employed and had not yet received his first paycheck. We both put our money together and had enough to fill my tank and get on the road.

When we got there the nurse told us that it wouldn't be long. I went in and kissed her and thanked her for all that she had given me. I didn't say anything to her that I had not already said before; I just wanted to be by her side when she closed her eyes. By 7am she passed and the nurse came and got me from a room that they had prepared for me and my brother to sleep in. I went to see her and she looked like she was asleep.

My grandmother died seven years and two days after my mother. This was eerie to me because I was already focusing on 2007 being my year of the completion of my mother's death, so for my grandmother to pass so close to my mother's death day was taken as a sign from God that everything was going to be all right. Ironically, she passed at 7am on the nose.

My grandmother and grandfather had a husband and wife suite at the rest home so when she passed he was alone in the room. Before the mortuary came to get my grandmother's body, I asked my grandfather if he wanted to see my grandmother. He said, "Why do I want to see a dead body?" At that time I knew he wasn't taking it well, but I asked him again if he wanted to see her; this time he said yes. When they rolled my grandmother's body over to him, I could see that his heart was broken; this was the woman with whom he had spent 68 years. She was his best friend and now she was gone. When they took her body away, the tears just rolled down his face.

The next day my aunt, uncle, sister, and I went to the funeral home to make the funeral arrangements. Because my grandparents had already paid for their graves and final arrangements, there was no financial burden on us. We just had to choose a day for the services. I wanted to do her hair and make-up, so I had to go to the funeral home on that Wednesday before the funeral, which was on Friday.

I had done my mother's make-up when she died, so I knew I had the courage to do my grandmother's. I still could not be alone so I asked my sister to come with me. I knew she didn't want to come but I begged her, I just could not do it alone. She finally agreed to come with me.

She did not look like herself, understandably. There was no spirit, it was just a shell. My grandmother always had her hair together since she was a hair stylist and hair weave specialist. I found some hair extensions that matched her hair, gave her extensions, and cut it into the style she always wore. After that I did her eyebrows and make-up just the way that she would have done; she looked beautiful. I was satisfied with the way that she looked and hoped that my family felt the same way.

The next day was Thursday and our family had to be there at ten o'clock in the morning to have last looks before the Quiet Hour, so our immediate family met in a small room that Fouche's had prepared for us. When my uncle arrived and saw her, he hugged me and said, "Oh Stacy, she looks beautiful. God is going to bless you." I broke down into tears because I did what I was supposed to do for her, not looking for any type of reward. My grandmother taught me how to do hair and kept my hair up every two weeks religiously as a child, so that was least that I could for her final arrangements.

The funeral service was held the next day, Friday, June 22, 2007. We began the service with our immediate family: the kids, grandkids, and the great grandchildren lead the praise and worship. After that I sang the Lord's prayer and "His Eyes Are On The Sparrow". It was truly a home going celebration; I could not figure out why I was so happy but yet so sad at the same time. I was happy that she was free of her sick body, but sad she was leaving me. It hit me all at once at the funeral especially when it was my turn to view her body. I went to the casket and kissed her and said my good byes, then when I sat down I suddenly got back up and went back to the casket and broke down. That was the last time I was going to be able to touch her and see her.

I know that she was with me in spirit which was the best but I just wanted to see her again and to look at my great work; I couldn't believe how good she looked.

In the midst of all the sadness, you know it is good to find humor to heal the spirit, and this time we didn't have to look far. My cousin Jeanette, whose hands have always been quick when it came to putting us in our place in church, was on her way to view my grandmother's remains. Her grandson was horse-playing by the casket, and the the next thing we knew we heard a SLAP! She had sally-boned her grandson in the head so loudly that it echoed in the church. What made it even worse was that he grabbed the back of his own head while walking away from the casket with a crazy look on his face. We all fell out! I am sure the church members thought we were all crying because my grandmother was gone. It was hilarious.

My brother-in-laws motorcycle club escorted the funeral procession, and since it was my turn to pay my sister back for the favor of coming to the mortuary with me to do my grandmother's hair, I rode in the hearse with the body. I don't know how I did it. Love truly conquers all fears, and our family friend Mr. Roy Northington was driving the hearse, which made things a bit easier.

After we came back from the funeral, everybody went to see my grandfather at the convalescent hospital. He could not come to the funeral because he was paralyzed from the waist down from cancer. I was so drained that I did not go with my family. I had to lay down and just take it easy; I was going to drive back to

LA the next day with my sister and brother.

We pulled out at about eleven o'clock that next morning and headed back to LA. By the time we got there, six hours later, my grandfather had passed. I was in shock. I could not believe it. My grandfather was now gone, too. I just thought I would lie down and die myself. Here I was, now faced with another death. For the third time in my life I had mixed emotions. I was happy that he was no longer suffering from prostate cancer and the fact that he and my grandmother were together again in less than a week, but it was a bittersweet feeling to see them go. They were the pioneers of our family, the ones who kept us together, and now they both were gone.

My sister and I felt that turning around to go back to Oakland was out of the question; we needed a break from funeral planning and decided to stay in LA and attend the BET awards that following Tuesday.

My sister had been coming to LA in past years to work the BET awards as a talent escort for Cossette Productions. Cossette Productions is the production lead for all the awards ceremonies; they provide the seat fillers, escorts, and volunteer staff for the award shows. I decided to go along with her, and even though I was not signed up with the company to escort, I went anyway and was able to sign up and actually work. It was a humbling experience for me because I had to follow celebrities around and make sure they were comfortable and in their respective places during the show. This was a learning experience for me too, because I got a chance to see just how ugly some entertainers are. Artists were showing up fashionably late to rehearsal and then would leave to go get food; it was horrible.

One thing that I learned is that before you see these award shows, there is *a lot* of work that goes on behind the scenes. I now have a great respect for the production of all of the award ceremonies; three days of prep work just so you, the viewer, see a great show. This was my first time escorting with my sister, and I truly thought that because this was my first time escorting that I would get a B or C list artist. I got Rocsi Diaz from 106 and Park! I was shocked, but nonetheless ready for the task. I found out the night before at rehearsal that my job was to make sure I knew where her seats were so that I could get her to the stage when she needed to be there. I had to learn how to operate my headsets that we would be communicating on, and got briefed on security issues. It was amazing to see how things all come together behind the scenes. I also learned that it's nice to be respectful and come in on your call time on time, otherwise it really messes things up with the show and timing.

It was really good to take my mind off of my own personal reality, but deep in my heart I knew that I had to face yet another death that I did not see coming so soon.

The day of the BET awards show my sister called me over on the radio to come to Talent Check-in at the Shrine. When I got there, she was standing with this guy and asked me "Do you know who this is?" I almost freaked out! It was Michael "Huggy" Carter from my mother's group "The Nine Lives". He still looked the same. He had added on a few pounds, but ultimately he still looked the same. I asked him who was he with and he told us that he was now Eve's road manager, and that he also managed Rihanna, Chris Brown, and Mary J Blige. He also indicated that he lived in Atlanta. I was so happy to see him still in the industry. Somehow, Huggy didn't know that my mother had passed in 2000, so we broke the news to him; he was shocked.

It was amazing to me how many people I knew backstage that were heavy hitters in the show. I knew Rihanna's bass player and manager, along with high security staff to background dancers and singers. I remember feeling some kind of way; I felt like it was supposed to be me going on stage singing background or better yet as an artist performing. I thought that these artists were no better than I, but also had to remember that "everyone has their time to shine" so I had to be patient.

I ended up being a talent escort for the next four years with Cossette, and had the chance to work with some great artists and icons. One particular Grammy show I worked with Stevie Wonder. Working with him was a blast; it was so amazing to me how he maneuvered and made his way around. I remember when they gave me my envelope with the name of the artist I was working with all weekend, I almost fell out! I looked up to the heavens and said, "Mom, you are showing out!" The next day I met him and his family, and the rest is history. I said, "Hi Stevie, I'm Stacy and I'll be at your service this weekend." He said, "What's your sign?" I said, "Virgo." He turned to his assistant and said, "She's Stacy, a Virgo. Ya dig!" I fell out laughing; that was best weekend of my life. I got a chance to hang out and be personable with my idol. Wow, I still pinch myself sometimes.

After meeting your assigned artist, it's then time to find their seats so that you know where to seat them during the show. Well, I was running around in the Staple Center looking for Stevie Wonder's seats and couldn't find them; I got so frustrated. I wanted to be on my job and have everything lined up. I finally went to my boss and said, "I can't find Stevie's seats." He looked at me and turned pink. While laughing, he said, "Stevie never sits in his seats." I asked why. He said, "Do you really think he watches the show?" I felt so ignorant. I thought about it and said, "You know, now that I think about it, I have never seen Stevie sitting in the audience at anything, he's always on stage." That was a fun fact that I quickly learned that weekend at the Grammys.

My god brother and childhood friend were performing that year with Mick Jagger and Raphael Sadiq. When working with production there are rules you must abide by in order to keep a professional relationship between artists and escorts. You cannot take pictures with them, you can't ask them for autographs; you have to keep it very professional and upright. After working with Cossette for four years, I knew the protocol and the rules which is why they would put me and my sister with A list artists every year. We knew how to conduct ourselves around celebrities. After getting Stevie settled, I stepped out of his dressing room that was right near the stage and I saw my god brother getting ready to hit the Grammy stage with two icons. When he saw me he said, "Stay, (his name for me), take this picture right quick!" Immediately I grabbed his camera and took a picture of him walking up the stage with Raphael and Mick; it was classic! I was overjoyed that somebody I knew and grew up with was on stage that night. As a matter of fact, a host of people I knew were on stage that night.

Later after the Grammys were over, my boss approached me and said, "Where is the camera?" I said, "What camera?" He grabbed my bag and began to search for a camera I didn't have. I realized right away what he was talking about. I explained that my god brother was going on stage and asked me to get a picture of him. Someone told the big boss that I was taking pictures of celebrities and their band members. I could not believe what I was hearing; someone actually went out of their way to have me reprimanded for taking a picture for my god brother. I began to get upset but I quickly gained my composure and told my boss that it's really not my fault who I know and who I'm associated with. I explained to him that growing up in the industry is how I knew these people and if that's too much for Cossett I understood, but I absolutely couldn't help who I knew. That was my last year of escorting, and I wasn't mad at all. In my heart, I knew I'd be back one day, but this time I'd be checking in as talent.

One week later we were back at it. I felt like I was in a dream state. Just last Friday I was saying goodbye to my grandmother and now I was saying goodbye to the man I knew as "Papa", a good provider, awesome protector, and all around good man. The service was great; we opened up with praise and worship with Alfreda Lions. I sang the Lord's prayer, Pastor Hunter did the eulogy, and we laid my grandfather to rest on top of my grandmother.

The next day I remember feeling anxiety because I still had my own issues to deal with on top of grieving. My house was foreclosing, and I thought my world was closing in on me. I had a few breakdowns, but not in front of my daughter. Somehow I managed to keep a smile on my face. I began to be proactive and started looking for a place to rent. I had no luck at finding a place because of my foreclosed property; it had been added to my credit profile. I went to the most run down places and was still denied a place to stay! This was devastating to me; I had never been turned down to rent anything. I was one of the people who foreclosed at the beginning of the housing crisis in California; this was before all of the bail out programs were created.

My biggest fear had manifested; I had no place to go, no one to turn to but God. I thought, "God, why have you forsaken me?" My daughter was in her last nine weeks of school and was preparing for state testing which meant I could not take her out of school. There was no other option but for me to stay in a hotel. We stayed at the Extended Stay America in Valencia, California. Instead of feeling down on myself, I turned that negative energy into thanks. I began to thank God for still blessing me; I had a roof, a kitchenette to cook food, and, thank God, the money to pay for a hotel. Even though I was displaced, I was not in the streets! Thank God.

After six weeks and $2,000 later, God still kept me. Eventually my sister called me and said, "Stacy, just come with Jaelyn. You can stay with me." My brother didn't have a place to go either, so he decided to come back to Oakland with his new baby. I begged my brother not to go back to Oakland. I told him Oakland was either death or jail for him. He said, "Why did you curse my life?" I wasn't cursing his life, I was only being real with what I knew of the statistics in Oakland. At that time gun violence was rampant and people were dying senselessly every day – there were 100-179 murders a year.

I drove back home to Oakland. I had not thought about coming home ever, but for some reason I knew that I needed to regroup and get my life straight. I thought, what better place to heal than home? It was time for me to get myself together and clean myself up. I could no longer let this drug take over my life and tear me down. I don't know how I fell so hard and ended up in this space, but it was horrible! I fell to the power of addiction and let it ruin my life. I was four weeks clean and headed back to what I called home.

Back row: my Aunty Gwen, Uncle George, and my mom.
Bottom: my grandfather Isaiah Randolph Jr., my grandmother Gladys Randolph, and my great grandfather Pa Isaiah Sr.

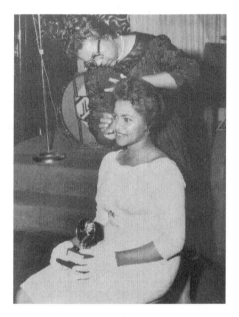

My grandmother styling our cousin Janice after she won a hair competition. It's amazing how much I look like her.

66

My mother and my Aunty Gwen standing in front our salon " Style Rite Beauty Salon"
1955

My parents at the prom as husband and wife. My mom had my older sister in her tummy.
1970

This is my dad's mother and father Richard and Velva Hogg.

1973! Sherron Hogg became a big sister!

1978. I was ready for business! This is me shampooing my older sister at the shampoo bowl

Before mom left For Japan

The band "9 Lives".This was their promotion picture for the tour in Japan

Mama on stage in Japan

Me with my first grade class in Boston, MA 1979

My senior picture from Skyline High School, Oakland

I graduated from junior college and went right into business for myself . My first salon -
2 Unique Hair in 1993.

My mom and I performing at my grandparent's 50th wedding anniversary. 1998

Our last family picture. 1999

2007-2007 my brother and I took this pic getting ready for our music project

Me, my brother, and sister on stage having a moment of silence for my mom. This was our last time on stage together

Me getting ready to sing the National Anthem for the Oakland A's MLB game for breast cancer awareness

2009, my brothers funeral. I sang one of our songs we had recorded together.

My first time back on stage without my mom and brother. I'm accompanied by my brother's daughter, Yanni.

Me and Oscar Grants uncle "Uncle Bobby" standing in solidarity for Alton Sterling.

Me and Oscar Grant's mom standing for justice for a 9 year old girl who was shot in Oakland

Me on stage at my event "Artivist Movement", 2015

My daughter with the president of the Boys and Girls Club of Oakland and Oakland's Mayor, Libby Schaaf.

Proud mom of a 2016 scholar, graduate, and teen pillar of society

V
Motherless Child

Oakland, CA. Back to where it all started for my family, back to the house where my mother took her last breath, back to the business where I learned how to do hair and become the woman I am. I was so overwhelmed by the fact that I was home, and now I had to really face my pain that I had been dealing with away from home. When I left Oakland, I felt like I was leaving the pain too, but all I did was mask it. As I walked through the dining room to get to the bedroom, I stood where my mother's hospital bed was and just stared into space. It took me back to June 16th 2000. I could actually feel my mother's embrace, and could hear her saying, "Welcome home, baby!" It was so real, I sighed and began to cry. I wanted to tell her everything I been through but for some reason I felt that she already knew, and she was the reason that I came back home. For weeks I could not stop sighing; it was like I had been through a fight and the fight was finally over, but little did I know the fight had only just begun. Sometimes you have to know when to let go and start over. I was drowning in debt and was in way over my head in bills.

I was glad to see my brother, although I had told him that I didn't think he should have come back to Oakland. The neighborhood that I knew as a child was plagued with murders every other day and included children as young as a year old! It was like there were no rules to the streets anymore; it used to be that you could not shoot women, children, or the elderly. Apparently, the new generation did not get that memo. My daughter could not play on the very streets I played on as a child, and this was baffling to me. How did my community get to this point? What happened? I found a Boys and Girls Club in West Oakland so that she could get some recreation time in for the summer, but soon found it that it, too, was in a high crime area. At this point I felt hopeless. I stepped out on faith and took her there anyway. I would pray for God to cover her and keep her in my absence. It helped that I knew one of the main directors. We grew up together and ran in the same circles in past years, and he said he would keep an extra eye on her for me which made me feel better.

Three weeks passed and I was involved in a horrible car accident. My car was totaled and I was without transportation for the first time in years. Just when I was feeling like things were almost coming together, here came more trials and tribulations on top of feeling frustrated and wondering how to climb out of this hole I had dug for myself. My finance company was looking for the car for nonpayment, and at the time of the accident I was not insured or licensed. I was penalized and my license was suspended for another three years. In years past I was able to buy cars with no license and continue to drive, but something about what I was coming out of and headed to made me stop and realize that this time I could not follow the same patterns that I was used to. When you want to grow, you have to stretch yourself and sometimes that's not easy. I chose the hardest thing to do and that was face the reality that I was a pedestrian for the next three years until my driving privileges were reinstated. Living displaced, and without transportation, made me feel like the walls were closing in on me.

After getting my daughter in school that fall she too went through her own adjustment after coming to Oakland; she had never been raised there. We left when she was two years old, and most of her elementary school years were in Glendale and Santa Clarita, CA. She was happy that she finally went to school with kids that looked like her, but they didn't talk like her. She was teased and bullied to the point that she tried to start talking slang to fit in. I heard my daughter say 'hecka' and I almost lost my mind! 'Hecka' is the alternative word for 'hella', slang that's pretty much indigenous to the Bay Area. I immediately asked her who taught her that word. I had to remind myself that 'hecka' is an Oakland word; you can go anywhere, state to state, and if they hear you say 'hecka' they know you're from the Bay Area. I had to check myself! Needless to say, she was going through an identity crisis and I had to work with her through it. I became a parent liaison and was at the school every day helping her transition to an all black school from a predominantly all white school. In LA, I was always at her school and I didn't want that to change. My Uncle George would take us to her school and I would walk back home after.

I was so concerned and consumed with what other people would think, I would dress like I was working out so that if anyone saw me walking, they would think I was exercising. I would go as far as jogging and fast paced walking just to make it look that way.

I had no clientele and I was out of the loop in terms of what styles people were wearing at the time. For the last eight years of my life, I was replacing hair and once a hair replacement client's hair is restored, they're really not too interested in the latest styles, they're just happy to have hair. I really didn't have a drive to do normal hair styles because it was more work and less money. I was used to making much more money practicing hair replacement.

My attitude about being home was so poor; this was not the way it was supposed to be. Although I had a roof over my head, it wasn't my roof. I sat in my room and asked God why He was forsaking me. Why did He take everything from me? My car, my house, my business...how could He love me? After crying and praying and more crying I began to sit quietly; it was like God was laying right next to me. His words were clear. He said "I provided you with a place to stay and a place to work." I sat there and thought, "Wow! You did, God. OK, I hear you, God!" I eventually went into our salon downstairs after two months and located a couple of old appointment books. I called old clients to let them know that I was back in town and if they needed my services, I was available. I got maybe two or three clients to come back, but not enough for me to move and get back on my feet.

I eventually had to go to Social Services for help. This was a most humbling experience. How did I go from making $65,000 a year to nothing? I was so mad at myself for letting my life slip through the cracks.

It was 2008 and most people were losing their jobs and homes. There was a high murder/suicide rate among married couples, especially in LA. I had never seen anything like this in my life. Welfare was not prepared to help people that were already educated and had skills. When I went into the social services office, the worker asked me what my skills were and I told her I was a licensed professional. I had experience in sales and marketing, and I was a recording artist. I gave her my business card. She looked at it and said, "I know you want a business, but you're not there yet." I wanted to tell her that I had been in business for myself since 1994, and who was she to tell me where I am? The nerve of her. I was ready to walk out and leave the building, but I had to stay. I had no other options. After doing tons of paperwork, I was finally done. I was asked to come back the next day for a "How to Dress for Success" interview class. The next day I showed up in my Calvin Klein two piece suit! I was looking better than the woman who was teaching the class. She looked at me and told me that I could go home. This woman could not teach me anything about how to go get a job! I just left a corporation where they hired me as their consultant and technical stylist for hair replacements; this welfare thing was a waste of my time. They were trying to send me to training to work at a J-O-B? NEVER, I told them. I am a licensed professional. I graduated from junior college with a skill set that no one could take from me. I told them to find me some clients - that's about all they could do for me. I absolutely was not going to go into training for something I wasn't going to do. The Welfare to Work program was a great program if you did not have a skill or didn't graduate from high school and did not have any training. For me it was a no go; I was not going to give up my love for styling and non-surgical hair replacement to work in someone else's office. It just wasn't going to happen. I did not come this far in life to regress, I only needed help getting back on my feet.

I was denied for services because I did not go through the training, but I didn't give up. I continued to submit my claim and eventually they put me on CalWorks, working under my own business. It wasn't easy and I had to fight them on this matter. In 2008, there were people down and out that had master's degrees and were highly educated losing their jobs and material gains. It was almost like the policies had to be redone because they no longer fit the one size fits all criteria. I had skills, I knew how to dress for success, and I had a business. I had an education, so where did I fit? It was a long battle but I fought hard and was victorious.

My clientele was not what it used to be, and I was only getting calls every blue moon. The money I was making was pennies compared to what I was used to making just months before.

I was trying to fight depression but everything around me was making me depressed, every day someone was being shot in my community. I came home one day and two guys were sitting in a car blocking our driveway. I thought to myself about how rude these people were, and I went into the house. Ten minutes later a car turns onto my block and the guys got out of the car and shot the man's car up with at least thirty bullets. The poor man did not stand a chance. He was hit by the hail of bullets and crashed into a pole down the street. I was not used to our community being like this; I didn't sign up to live in a war zone. Every other day kids were being killed. I had to stop looking at the news; it was so heart wrenching seeing mothers cry on TV begging the community for help. I consumed myself with what was going on around me. I was afraid, depressed, and had no drive to do anything.

My brother moved back to Oakland before I did with his girlfriend and daughter. I was so upset when he left LA because I had worked so hard to get him out of the environment that was not conducive for him in Oakland. I fought the California Parole Board tooth and nail for them to parole him to LA so that he could rehabilitate himself after being in prison for three years. But he actually surprised me; he enrolled in Chabot College and was looking to start a career in film.

Sedric knew what I had just come out of and knew that I was depressed. One day he called me crying and said, "I'm working on a song that reminds me of Mom." I didn't have a car so I said, "Come get me." He and my cousin Kalib picked me up; we went back to our studio and recorded "23rd Psalms". He created a track and the rest was history! We finished that song in an hour. I had been telling my brother to sing more because he had an amazing voice. Not only could he rap but he could harmonize and sing as well. He thought about what I said and he eventually put some harmony on my vocals and added an ad lib track. The song was perfect! After we finished our session, my brother looked at me and said, "I'm going to give you my password for the computer with all the music on it." I wondered why he was giving me his password, but didn't question it.

About a month later, my brother started making five beats a day and would come to my house, giving me CD's and saying, "I just finished this track. I need you to write to this." I would take the songs, listen to them, and never picked up a pen or pencil. I was not in a creative space at all, how could I be? I was clouded with depression, and guilt from the past. I had no desire to write because I didn't know what to say; no matter how hard I tried I could not be creative. The CD's kept coming and I kept stacking them up. We had recorded five songs in LA that were not complete so we were trying to complete those songs too, but between his school schedule and me trying to pull myself out of depression, we kept hitting and missing.

A few weeks later I had heard about an Oakland A's game that was honoring survivors of breast cancer. The game was on my birthday, September 5th. I called the A's business office and asked if I could do a fundraiser for my organization that day. They agreed and gave me the details regarding ticketing and pricing. I later found out that one of my high school classmates worked for them, so I emailed him and asked if I could sing the national anthem and honor my mother and the organization for the game. I was asked to send a demo of me singing the national anthem and they would decide later. Two weeks later I received the call from Warren Choo congratulating me on being chosen to sing the anthem for the game. I was on a spiritual high! This was the high that I had been looking for all along.

***

September 5th 2009. It was the day of the game, and we had to be there early because the breast cancer event actually started hours before the game. We had a Sharon Randolph Foundation booth, and we handed out information on our organization's mission and what programs we offered to women suffering from cancer. I sold over 40 tickets to the game. Most of the sales were to my own family; I was so happy to have my

84

brother and sister there. While I was getting my make-up done they both were manning our booth. Later, someone came and got me on a golf cart so that I could do a sound check. I had sung the national anthem at an NBA Golden State Warriors game in 1999, but it was indoors. This was my first time singing in an outdoor stadium. When I began to sing, my voice kept bouncing back at me, it was so weird! I had to keep focused on what I was singing because the timing would have thrown me off. It was a great sound check, I was ready to go! At the beginning of the game, they had me walk out with over 500 breast cancer survivors in pink Oakland A's shirts. It was awesome. The ladies stayed on the field in a large circle while I sang. As I was singing, I looked up over the batting cage and my sister was right there, capturing the moment on film. I was nervous and scared, but at some point I just focused on the fact that I was there representing my mother, and somehow that fear left me. It was almost like her spirit came through me and said, "Baby, you got this!" Two minutes later I was done and had one more accomplishment to add to my resume. Security then escorted me to my section that was set up for me and my guests, and when I got there all of my family stood up and cheered me on. For the first time in a long time I was feeling good. I missed the entire game because people were asking me for my autograph and wanted to take pictures with me. I can't tell you who won the game, but I do remember that it was close.

After the game, my brother sat with me and said, "Sister, you just sang in front of all of these people. Wow!" I told him, "Brother, this is only the beginning. We are going to do this, this is our life." When I got home, I had time to reflect on the day and how successful it was. Usually when I sing or perform I get this energy that keeps me up, I don't know what that is but it never fails. Needless to say, I was up all night.

The next day a good friend of mine took me and my sister out to eat. It was still my birthday weekend and I was accepting all invitations to celebrate my life. We ate, and afterwards my friend saw a guy that he knew and introduced both me and my sister to him. He said, "Meet Derrick Bedford. This dude is the man to know. He has an awesome story of resilience." He went on to say that this brother was headed for destruction and had been fighting a criminal case that he not only won, but it was dropped. Soon after, he changed his life and was now working on the other side of the law. He now worked as a supervisor at juvenile hall in Alameda County. The same courtrooms he was in and out of as an offender were now the place where he stood for at-risk youth. When my sister and I heard his story, we immediately thought about our brother. We exchanged numbers so that we could introduce Sedric to him. My brother's story was parallel to his story; my brother had recently changed his life and was setting out to help others in the community discover a different perception of life. Sedric was working on a DVD called 16 Bars; he basically was trying to bridge the gap between East and West Oakland rappers. Each artist in the video had 16 Bars, no more no less, to tell their story of what they saw in the streets of Oakland on a daily basis. I rushed his number to my brother and told him to set up an appointment with him so that he could show him his DVD, and possibly discuss how the video could be used to bring the community together. I was excited for my brother because it had not been easy for him. He was finally doing something positive to bring about change.

***

Thursday September 10th, 2009. My brother came over to show me his DVD packaging and I hit the roof! He was handing out CD's with no labels on them; it looked like he had just burnt 50 plain CD's to hand out. It was not a reflection of how we do business and I didn't want him to sell the DVD looking like that. I said, "Sedric, you can't present that to anybody in a blank slip cover, put your label on it!" We started arguing back and forth with each other. I asked him why he didn't ask me for the money to help, and he said, "Because I'm a MAN! You and Sherron always help me; I just want to be a man and do this on my own." Eventually my uncle came out of his room and said, "Stacy, listen to Sedric. Sedric, listen to Stacy. You both have valid points but listen to each other." At that moment, we brought it down a notch and listened to each other. All I wanted him to understand was that first impression is the key and Mama taught us better than that. All he was trying to say to me was that he wanted to be a man and not have to ask for help from me and my sister. We hugged each other and walked to the store, and I don't know why but I thanked him for all the support he gave me while I was going through addiction. He said, "Sister, it's OK. I understand." I insisted, "No, I have to thank you because you were there to bring me back into my love for music and you were my support system. So, thank you!" We laughed and that was the end of that.

The next day I was preparing to go to my best friend's brothers' wedding in Napa. I didn't have a car so my sister said that she would come get me and take me to Vallejo where she lived. Napa was only 30 minutes from her house. By the time my sister came, my brother showed up at the same time, got out of his car and said, "I did it!" He had labels on the DVD and slip covers that said '16 BARS'. I said, "Yes!!! This is how we do business, brother. I'm proud of you!" He went on to say that he had made the appointment with Mr. Bedford and they were going to meet on Sunday. Both me and my sister begged him to not be late, and to call him if he was going to change his plans. He agreed, we both said "I love you" and drove our separate ways.

***

Saturday September 12th, 2009. The wedding was absolutely beautiful; it was my first time going to a wedding in Napa. The winery overlooked the vineyards and mountains, it was nice. During the wedding my phone rang and I didn't answer it because the wedding was in progress, so I sent the call to voice mail. Later, after the wedding, I forgot to call the number back; it was party time and we were having fun. It was nice to be around my bestie and her family. They moved from California in 1993 and I don't think I saw her in all that time. I was having a ball; our mutual friend picked me up from my sister's house and offered to take me back after the reception. My phone had dead, and I was not receiving calls by the end of the night. We eventually got on the road headed back to my sister's house. When we pulled up, I noticed that the front door was wide open and the lights were out. I walked in the house and was immediately confused as to why the door was open and it was dark. My first thought was that someone had broken into the house, but where was my daughter and my sister? I walked out and went to the car to get the rest of my things and Shamika said, "Your sister just called and wants me to take you home." I was so confused; I can't tell you what was going through my mind. It was about 2am Sunday morning. When we pulled up to my house, the lights were on and several cars were parked in front of the house. I knew something wasn't right. When I walked through the door, the living room was full of family members. I looked around and did not see my baby. I screamed, "JAELYN! Where is my baby?" My sister stood up and said, "Jaelyn is fine, she's in bed." I asked where my uncle was. She said he was in his room. By this time I knew somebody was dead because I had ten family members in my living room and it was 2am. No one wanted to say anything. Finally Sherron cried out, "They killed our brother!" I dropped to the ground and started screaming at the top of my lungs, "I'M SORRY, MAMA!"

All I could think about at that moment was the fact that I had promised my mother on her death bed that we would make sure my brother would be OK. I felt like I failed her; how could I let her down in her absence? I really felt like my mother was with us, not realizing that he was now in the spirit world with her. I was in disbelief that he was gone, and struck with immediate grief! I cried. I asked questions. Who, what, when, where, and lastly WHY? I later found out that he was helping my cousin set up his studio in Acorn Projects in West Oakland. After he finished putting the studio together, he left and realized that he left behind a memory stick. He went back to my cousin's house to get his things, and when he got out of the car he was shot eleven times. I made my cousin Rachelle take me to the crime scene and that was not a good idea. When we drove up I saw my brother's blood still on the streets! I was a wreck. I just screamed and hollered, "WHY?!" They took me home and I cried myself to sleep.

The next morning, Mr. Bedford called my sister and I and asked, "Where is your brother? He was supposed to be here at 9am." I dropped the phone. I was numb. I could not utter the words, "He got shot." My sister picked up the phone and said, "Derrick, my brother was murdered." He was shocked! He gave us his condolences, and said to not hesitate to give him a call if we needed anything. Now this was surely life changing for me and could be the very thing that made me relapse back on drugs. I could not face this type of pain; I needed to mask this pain and I didn't want to face the fact that my little brother had just been murdered. I didn't really have the urge for narcotics so I just drank myself under the table.

In the hood people talk, but I was the victim this time so nobody talked to me. I immediately went to my little play sister who had an ear to the streets and I told her to find out what happened to my brother. I didn't care how she did it, I just needed her to find out. I needed the truth! I had to focus on laying my brother to rest; I couldn't be McGruff the Crime Stopper so I had other people doing investigations for me.

Monday morning we called the coroner's office so that we could start making plans for his funeral services. Clearly, I was not the person to handle business because when they said there would be an $85 processing fee to release his body, I hit the roof! Homicides are big business. By the time we got his body to the mortuary, we were already out $100.

As days went by, I began to lose trust in everybody. I didn't know who murdered my brother, I didn't know why, and I found myself calling my cousin and drilling him like a drill sergeant. I knew my brother was not into the street stuff because between his class at Chabot College and living in the lab making beats, he had no time to be involved in criminal activity.

A few days before the funeral my niece Yanni and her mom Amber came up from LA, and when I saw my niece I became totally undone. I had to look at my niece's innocent face, knowing she would not ever see her daddy again. I looked up at Amber and said "I'm sorry." When we lived together in LA after she had given birth to my niece, and my brother was doing everything but breast feeding the baby. I eventually told her, "Look, you have got to start trying to do things around the house." I told her that my brother was not promised to be around all the time. I didn't mean it like this though; I was thinking more in terms of if they didn't make it as a couple she would have to do this on her own. We cried, gave each other hugs, and I promised her that we would continue to be in my niece's life, no matter what.

My sister and I made an executive decision to have everyone wear jeans and white T's and/or a white shirt. We also made the decision to have Derrick Bedford (also known as DB) to do my brother's eulogy. We could have had our pastor, Pastor Hunter, do the eulogy but we thought that because most of my brother's friends were from the streets, it would be good to have someone that could relate to them speak. His story and testimony alone would give them hope for a brighter day.

All week leading up to his funeral, the 1400 block of Campbell Street was packed. His friends started a mural and people were coming to sign it. I think it was a white sheet that was put on the wall. The day of the funeral I took it down and folded it up as if it was a flag, like they do with deceased veterans, and I put it in his casket before the funeral started. He *was* a veteran to me; he survived these ugly streets and the racism that plagues our community among other black men. He had to fight against just being a black man living on earth.

His funeral was tailor made for him. He actually performed at his own service - we played the 23rd Psalms song that he and I had just finished months before. I then sang a song that we wrote to one of his tracks. We didn't have a choir and we didn't read resolutions like a traditional funeral; we made people that would not normally come to church feel welcomed. I didn't want anyone turned away, and I didn't want his friends feeling like they had to dress up. We had to meet them where they were and we did. DB delivered a great eulogy and we ended the service. The recessional song was our other song that we recorded, "Mama Said". As I listened to the song, it took me back to the studio in Arizona where we recorded it, and all I could see was his face while we were in the vocal booth as he told me, "You can do this part better." I got up and went to the microphone and started singing with the CD. By the time the song was over the church was empty. I continued to sing to the very end of the song. The limo driver came into the church and said, "We are ready to go." I was the only person unaccounted for in the limo. It was so funny. Everyone was

90

looking at me like, "Get it together, Stacy." Once we got to the cemetery, his plot was on a hill and most people would not be able to stand on the edge, so the committal was done along the path that lead to his grave. Once the committal was over and they lowered him into the grave, I saw my sister lean over his casket and just lay there. I was totally undone at this point. I knew what she was feeling; this was our baby brother that my mother brought home to us, and now we were laying him to rest at the same cemetery as my mother. Afterwards, I went to visit my mother's grave and said, "Mom, your baby is right up the hill", I felt closure of some kind. I felt that my sister and I had laid my brother to rest exactly how he would have wanted us to. The real battle was yet to come, yet again.

Weeks later I fell into a deep depression. I woke up every morning, drank a bottle of champagne, and went to sleep with a bottle at night. I started making all kinds of flavored mimosas and didn't realize that this was a problem until one day I looked up and saw over ten empty champagne bottles I had collected in my kitchen in less than a week. I was taking down two to three bottles a day. I sat in my room and didn't go anywhere but to church. Somehow I still felt like I needed God more than ever at this point. I drowned myself in grief with alcohol to keep myself from going back to cocaine. I didn't want that type of high, I just wanted to ease the pain but that never happened. I went into seclusion, and had a fear that something was going to happen to me next. I felt that our community had no hope, that this black on black crime was not going to get any better. It seemed as though every time I turned on the TV, there was a parent or family on the news crying, asking the community for their help because their loved one had been murdered. This too made me depressed because I knew exactly how they felt - getting that call and being told that your loved one was gone. During this time, the Oscar Grant case in Oakland was heating up. Oscar Grant had been killed on New Year's Day, 2009, by a BART (Bay Area Rapid Transit) police officer. I followed the case closely.

Not having transportation was the other issue that had me depressed. I was too afraid to be around people in public. I went through this for about two years, and I was tired of it.

**

2010. We were getting ready to finally move out of my grandparent's house. We cleaned it up so that we could rent it out. While cleaning the house, I found my childhood 10-speed bike along with my grandfather's classic Schwinn 10-speed. My bike unfortunately was damaged from being in the basement for twenty years, but my grandfather's bike was in good condition. I cleaned it up and chose to ride a bike in place of catching the bus. I had gained over 50 pounds; I needed the exercise anyway. Besides, riding a bike would not look like I didn't have a car; my ego was still in control and I didn't want to look bad. I wanted to look good from the outside. I got up in the morning and rode my bike to the bank, and all the places I needed to go to run errands. I joined Club One Gym (a high-end sports club) that catered to my needs. I began to workout and get healthy. All of the alcohol I was drinking put weight on me, but how I afforded this luxury I don't know. The universe made it happen is all I can say. I finally had a regular routine.

I rode my bike regardless of the weather. I would ride my bike in the rain thinking, "God, I can't wait to be a licensed driver again." I put myself through this torture so that when I got my license I would appreciate it and not mess up again by disobeying the law by not having insurance and driving without a license.

One day I was riding my bike into town and I ran into my pastor. He was dropping his daughter off at a school nearby. I had tears in my eyes when I rode up to him and he asked if I was OK. I assured him that I was, but I was just thanking God for my two hands and two feet that allowed me to ride a bike. At that point it had become very clear to me to just be thankful for where I was right then so that I could be blessed with more. I was so humbled by having to ride a bike; I learned a lot in this lesson of life. I could not continue my old ways if I wanted to experience transformation and change. I had to do something different to get different results, and I did. I continued to pray and ask for strength, not to remove my situation but to give me strength to get through it. Trials build

92

character.

One day I was home and I tried to sing a song but could not open my mouth to sing, I was going through the same kind of depression when my mother passed. It hurt to sing; it gave me memories of my family being on stage together and that was too painful. One afternoon, my cousin Cathy called me; she had lost her son three months before my brother was killed. She said that her son, my cousin, and my brother came to her in a dream, and my brother asked her to ask me what I was waiting for. I almost dropped the phone! I knew exactly what my brother was telling me: I'm still with you, let's finish this project! My brother had given me his password to his computer with his music on it, and I thought, OK, I'm ready to listen to the music he had left. It had been a whole year since he had passed and I desperately wanted to move out of the space I was in to a more happier and fulfilling life.

After going through most of his music, I found five tracks that I really liked and started writing. I figured I didn't have to sing to write, so I played the songs and just wrote how I felt. I came up with a song called "Motherless Brotherless Child". It felt good to write and get my feelings out on paper. I was writing about how losing my mother to cancer and losing my brother to gun violence made me feel. My brother and I had started working on our projects together in LA; we had songs that were ready to be recorded on top of the music he had been giving me once we both were home.

When I was in LA going through my storm - losing my first property, fighting addiction, and living with grief - there was a strong silent voice that told me, "Write a book and do a soundtrack." I started writing the book nine months before coming back home to Oakland. When my brother was killed, I had no drive to complete anything. I felt myself slipping back into the same kind of depression I had with my mom, and I had totally forgotten about what God said to do. I was determined not to go back to drugs and alcohol to mask my pain. I found Butch, our voice coach from the days when I sang in Image, and asked him to help me get my vocals in shape to record. I knew that Butch knew how to get me together and back to recording because he had done it before.

In my mother's absence, there was no better person to help train my vocals.

After four weeks of grilling songs and exercising my vocals, I felt strong enough to record. At first, I was focused on the things I didn't have and when I realized that my brother left me music I got busy and started working on what I *did* have in my life, I had music to write to, produce and record, and that's what I did. Blessings started flying out of the sky.

The principal at my daughter's school, Karen Haynes, was an advocate for students in the arts, and had a state of the art studio built in one of the school's classrooms. Ms. Haynes allowed me to bring my team there to record and start the pre-production process of my project. This was a blessing out of the heavens because I didn't have to pay for studio time or for pre-production work. This also allowed me to be at my daughter's school, to be present for her needs, and volunteer at the same time. I was killing three birds with one stone. While working on the pre-production, I was worried about how I was going to actually record the songs. I had been used to having our own studio to record out of when my brother was alive. This made me feel even more depressed; I now had to think about who would record it and where. A few weeks later I was in conversation with a good friend and he said, "Stacy, I believe in you. Don't worry, I will help." He gave me $1,000 to get the project going. If I had any doubt in my mind that this was what I was supposed to do, I could not deny it then. Everything I was making up excuses for was already being handled. I also had a relationship with Paula and Jim at Pajama Studios; this is where a lot of Bay Area musicians and singers recorded in Oakland - artists like En Vogue, Toni Tony Tone, Luniz, Too Short, you name it, they all recorded there. Besides, Jim Gardner, the owner, was a Grammy nominated engineer and composer. I was so happy to be home, finally getting back into loving the music again. It had been ten years that I had been MIA from the music industry and it was half due to the fact that I lost my drive and dedication to the craft. I knew this was what I needed for myself, but I still had doubt in what God had asked me to do. All I kept thinking was, "God, where am I supposed to get the resources to write a book

94

and do a soundtrack?" I was in my own way! When God asks you to do something, just do it! He is going to give you everything you need to accomplish His task. I was finally starting to realize this in my life.

I invited my father to come to the studio while I was recording. My father had never been to a recording studio ever in his life; he wasn't too interested in coming to the studio when I was recording in my 20's. I was so happy to have my daddy there watching me in action. He was amazed at how things worked in the studio, and he was recording me on video from his phone while I was recording. After the session was over, my father looked at Jim Gardner and expressed how amazing he thought all of that was. Jim asked, "You've never been to the studio and Stacy Hogg is your daughter?" I felt so bad for my dad because he couldn't answer that question. He had distanced himself from us so much that he didn't know the things that mattered to me, he didn't know what gave me drive. If he knew, he had never seen it in action. We went out to eat after, and my father said, "Stacy, you have your own sound and I think that's good that you don't sound like anybody else." I turned to him and asked, "Do I, Daddy?" I was like a little girl whose father had just validated her for the first time. He had never been to any of my live performances, but he had every rap song that I ever sang on, from Bad Influence and The Click to Ant Banks' TWDY CD. He was a fan, but from a distance. We had a great conversation that day; I needed to hear my father's validation. For the first time in my life, I felt what it feels like to have my father believe in me.

***

June 12th, 2012. I got a call from my extended niece, Janie, asking me to come to the hospital because her brother had been shot. I was still riding my bike and I knew I would not be able to get there fast enough so I called my sister to take me. By the time we got there, he had passed away from gunshot wounds to the chest. I was in immediate grief for the family. I watched this young man grow up and now another one of my close extended family members were gone. I thought, "God, I can't do this! Why did you bring me back to this madness in Oakland?" After the family decided that it was best to continue to grieve alone, we all gathered outside the hospital. His mother came to me and asked me if I could sing at his services and do his final looks, giving him a line and cleaning up his mustache. I assured her that she had me for whatever she needed done to lay her son to rest. By this time I had gotten my license but I was still without a car. I went to Rent-a-Relic and rented a car so that I could help with anything that was needed. The day before the funeral, I went to do his last looks at the funeral home and went by the house to check on the family. The next day was the funeral; it is never easy to bury loved ones and I have never had to bury a child so I was in deep grief for his mother. I could not relate to her pain, and yet I could relate to his sister's pain. I've buried a brother and it was painful. The service was a great home going service. His life was celebrated right.

Two weeks later his mother asked me to meet her for dinner at one of my favorite restaurants in Oakland, Kincaid's On The Water. There were about eight of us, and at the end of dinner she passed each and every one of us a card. We each opened the cards and read them individually out loud, and when it came time for me to read my card, I fell out! I opened up a pink slip and keys to a Toyota Camry. I literally passed out! Who hands you keys and a pink slip to a car? Lynn Chess blessed me with a car; I had no idea of the blessing that was coming my way, all I could do was cry and thank God for her and her heart. At the same time she was thanking me for my heart. All of the days that I was on a bike in the rain, and all the cold days when I didn't want to get on the bike but had to, it all made sense to me right at that moment. I had to sacrifice in order to be blessed and have God's blessings on my life. If I had been running around town driving on a suspended license, I would not have had God's blessings in my life because I would not have been a law abiding citizen while driving recklessly, with no drive to do better. Integrity is doing what is right even when no one is looking, and this was my first reward of having good integrity. Lynn, I can't thank you enough. You are truly a blessed woman.

I was finally on the road again and things were looking up for me. I was able to get myself to and from the studio, I was able to go to 8am service because the people who I had previously gotten rides with went to the 11am service. It was like becoming an adult all over again; I had my independence back, I could go where I wanted to when I wanted to, and in my own car.

***

September 26th, 2012. My sister called and said that my father was not answering the door, and that my Uncle Warren was at his house with the police. By the time I got there, the fire department had gone in and pronounced him dead. When they finally let us into the house, we discovered my father's body at the kitchen table slumped over with his calculator and checkbook in front of him with his cordless phone. My initial emotion was anger! How could he die worried about bills? Why was he up balancing his checkbook? My father was very systematic; he got up, made up his bed, and opened the blinds, in that order. His bed wasn't made, and his blinds were not open which meant that he woke up and went straight to his table and died. After a half hour of being mad, it finally dawned on me that my father was gone. I did not know how to feel. I would be so mad at my daddy that sometimes I would say, "What is he here for?" Our last time with each other was at the studio, and all I could do is go back to that moment when he said, "You got your own sound, go for it." But how? My mama, my brother, my grandparents, and now my father? I didn't want God to show how strong I was anymore! How am I supposed to heal from these deaths? It was like a wound with a scab on it that kept getting picked and it starts to bleed all over again. I was tired of opening and closing wounds.

It took the funeral home about three hours to come get his body, so we pulled out a bottle of Skyy vodka from his bar and turned on Marvin Gaye's "Keep on Dancing" and partied until they scooped him up.

Like all the deaths before, I turned to the bottle for comfort and solace. I had to watch my mother take her last breath, and I had to walk in and find my father at his kitchen table, stiff as a board. My last conversation with my dad was when he called me two weeks before he passed to remind me to pay the cleaning fee

97

for our vacation property in Las Vegas. He was such a worry wart; I always paid it, but every quarter I could expect a call from my father reminding me to pay it. Two days before his services, I did my father's last looks; I gave him a line and cut his hair. The next day we had to view him as a family. My uncles were there and both my grandparents. We did not know if my grandmother knew what was going on because she was in her final stages of Alzheimer's. Six hours later we got a call indicating that my dad's older brother, Wendell, had a massive stroke. "God," I thought. "I can't do this, this is too much for us to go through." My uncle could not go to his brother's funeral because he now was fighting for his own life. He and my father were very close and I imagine the stress of his brother being gone was too much for his body to handle.

My father's service was at the funeral home and we sent him out the way he lived. After the service was over we put on Marvin Gaye and danced out of the mortuary to the same song we played when the coroner took his body out of the house.

My father was very instrumental in helping my grandfather take care of my grandmother, and when he died I think both of my grandparents went into a depression. For my grandmother, the Alzheimer's got worse. My grandfather just gave up the will to live. Six month after the funeral, he started losing weight at a rapid pace and it became quite alarming. My Uncle Warren was the only one capable of taking care of my grandparents since my Uncle Wendell had a stroke. We took my grandfather to the hospital and they said he had lung disease. My grandfather was in his mid 80's and he didn't want to treat it, he didn't want surgery. I could tell after my father died that he just wanted to fade off. His garden started declining, the plants in the house were dying, and the yard was not kept up like he usually kept it. This showed me that it doesn't matter how old your children are, when you lose a child it affects you no matter what. Six months passed and we had to use my grandmother's in-home care nurse for both my grandfather and my grandmother.

Two months later I decided that I could not go on without getting professional help so I found a therapist and I attended sessions weekly. There was so much pain built up from grief, I knew that it was time for me to release and let go.

A good friend of mine worked out at the same sports club, and she invited me to take a course at the Landmark Forum. Landmark is a worldwide personal development and training program that provided me the tools to cut restraints and truly transform my life. After doing the work, I was able to be fully self-expressed; I regained my confidence, and most of all I was able to begin the healing process of what had been 40 years of distorted views and perceptions of life based on what I had seen in my journey. I was able to get a different perspective, and clean out space in my life that had been filled with unhealthy thinking, grief, resentment, shame, blame, and guilt.

***

November, 2014. I went to my grandparent's house. My grandfather was in and out, he would talk and then fall asleep. Somehow we got on a conversation about not letting people in that don't call first. The day before a lady from their church came over to bring my grandmother flowers for the house, and she didn't call before coming. My grandfather told me that he didn't open the door for people who didn't call before they came. We got into this big conversation about why you don't open the door for people that come to your house unannounced. I was so surprised because I am the same way, it's just a common courtesy to call before you show up to someone's house. After we finished that conversation, he looked up to me and said, "I need you to be here tomorrow." I got really nervous, and asked him why. Was it something he wanted me to do? In my mind I felt he wanted all of us at the house when he passed; I could feel he was ready to go. I assured him that I would be over the next day. I kissed him, told him I loved him, and left. By the time I got to the freeway my uncle called and told me to come back, my grandfather had just passed. I had only been gone five minutes! I knew he wasn't going to hold on much longer, but I had hope that he had one more day.

Back at the same mortuary, a year and two months later, I was making arrangements for my grandfather's home going. I was concerned that my grandmother didn't know what was going on, and when we walked into the mortuary to view his body, we rolled her wheelchair up to the casket and with a straight face, with no emotion, she said, "Look at my husband." That touched my heart so much, I was overjoyed that she knew who was laying there and I felt blessed that she really had no emotion. I don't think I would have been able to handle that. I was equally concerned about my uncle who had lost his brother and a now a year later lost his father. Our concern was that he would have another stroke.

We finally got through the service and burial, then we had to get my grandmother situated at home. When my grandfather was alive, they both had one nurse which was originally for my grandmother, and when my grandfather got sick we paid her double to take care of them both. She lived in their home to take care of them and continued living there after my grandfather passed. A month later I got a call from my uncle stating that he had to fire the in-home nurse for abusing my grandmother. He had cameras installed in the house and caught her on tape mishandling my grandmother. Good thing I had already started working on personal development at this point, because I was ready to take it to the streets! I still knew people from all lifestyles, I could have handled her in a way that would not have been good for her or her family. But I'm here to tell you, when you are caught in situations that you used to handle one way but no longer crave to revert to the past, that's when you know you have transformed. I actually prayed for the woman and left it in God's hands.

After going through that, we decided as a family that I would move in and take care of my grandmother. When Alzheimer's patients are in their final stages, it's good to keep them in their own home where they are familiar with everything. This gives them comfort and keeps them alive longer. My grandmother was in her final stages and I would get up in the mornings, clean her up, dress her, put her in her wheelchair and take her to the living room. Before I could get the curtains open she would ask, "Why are my curtains closed? Open my curtains, it's too dark in here." My grandparent's house overlooked the mountains and the city of Oakland so we had great views. She loved the view and still remembered that she had it. I was honored to take care of my grandmother, but it wasn't easy. This was the grandmother that spoiled me and both of my sisters. This was the grandmother that didn't make us lift a finger when we came over, all we had to do was be little princesses, and that was hard for me since I was a tom boy. My grandmother Gladys (my mother's mom) would have to deprogram me and Sherron after being at her house. We would come back home to my grandmother and she would ask us to wash the dishes or clean up. We would give her grief and get our behinds whooped!

My grandmother's bedroom was huge; we had a hospital bed in the room along with her queen-sized bed. This way I was able to be right there with her. As she got closer to the time of her transition, she would cry and moan at night. One night she started calling out for my father and my grandfather. I just sat up and cried. She wanted my daddy and her husband and they weren't there. I would get up and cut the light on for her so that she could see that I was there, and to my surprise my grandmother recognized me until the day she passed, six months later.

***

July, 2014. I woke up and the day nurse that relieved me for work came in that morning. By the time I got home my grandmother was transitioning. I knew because I recognized it from the experiences with my mother, both grandparents, and my grandfather. My uncle didn't really know, and I didn't say anything. I didn't want him to get scared or nervous. I called my sister Sherron and said, "Come over. Mama Velva is transitioning." By the time I got off the phone my grandmother looked at me and my uncle as if to say, "I love you guys" and transitioned into eternity. By the time my sister got there she was already gone, and I had to step out of the house because it was so overwhelming. Five minutes later I got a call from my sister.

"SHE'S DEAD!"

"I know. I told you she was transitioning!" I said.

"Transitioning where?"

"To eternity!" I exclaimed.

She hung up in my face and was mad at me, and I couldn't do anything but laugh hard. My sister had no idea she was walking in to say good bye to a cold body. In years prior, the phone call to my sister would have been so dramatic that she would have known my grandmother was passing because I would have said, "She's dying, come quick!" After personal development and training my language had changed and my sister was not used to the new me.

Here we were again, three years in a row at the mortuary making funeral arrangements again. This time going in, we knew exactly what to do. We said, "NO, we don't need a 'sealed tight', NO we don't need hair and make-up, I got that. NO, we don't need a quiet hour, and NO we don't need a limo." When you have buried as many people as I have, you become wise to the tricks and scams that are out there preying on families that are grieving. That's another book. However, we were prepared and it was easy because this set of grandparents had their final arrangements in order. It made the grieving process much easier. I felt so bad for my uncles, Wendell and Warren. They lost their brother and parents, three years in row. I had to look deep inside of my soul to get through this. All of my immediate family had left me. All that was left was me and my sisters, nieces and nephews. My mother died in June 2000, her parents together in June 2007, my brother in September 2009, my father in September 2012, my grandfather in November 2013, and my grandmother in July 2014. How do I get through this? I was at my wit's end. Two weeks later I went back to work.

Each death in my life was like a scab, it kept reopening every time someone else died. I tried to mask the pain with the bottle and it wasn't working. It was only making it worse; I was on a mission to crash and burn again and didn't realize what I was doing.

My uncle saw that I clearly needed a break and sent me and my daughter on an eight day vacation to Maui five days later. It was there that I started looking at everything I had been through in life, and realized that we have ups and we have downs and when we are in between those ups and downs, we have to be grateful and appreciative because we are alive. This life is a journey and no one ever said it would be easy. I got up each morning at 5am and ran on the beach. I would run and cry some mornings just giving God the praise for what He was about to do in my life. I joined the sports club at my resort and took a meditation course on the beach each morning. It was really awesome to meditate to real ocean sounds, and it was there that I chose to continue my education for personal development. I was tired of dealing with my grief. I was still grieving my mother when her parents died, I was grieving all of them. My brother's murder, and on top of that my father and his parents passing (who were very instrumental in my life), were all weighing on me so hard that I had no room to create. All of my creative space was taken up with anger, grief, sadness, disappointment, hurt, and depression. I was ready to get complete with the issues in my life and began to be active at fixing what wasn't working. I was ready to live the life I wanted, I was ready to be free of guilt and shame from my past. The things that were not working in my life were consuming me and blocking me from what I really wanted.

When I returned home from Hawaii I was energized and ready to hit the ground running. I enrolled in a self-development course and started the work on my life and personal development. It was there that I discovered that I am the possibility of love and compassion. I was able to clear the junk out of my life and create what was possible for me. I had to release blame, forgive myself, and finally let go of the past. I discovered that we really do focus on the past and future as if they exist right now. They don't, all we have is the present moment. If we live in the present we will find peace and joy by just living in the moment. I also discovered that I had created myself to be someone that I wasn't. My perception of who I was, was not the truth. All of my issues that I had been dealing with caused me to speak in a negative context to myself and listening to that negative voice made me feel as though I was not good enough, when in actuality I was.

The work that I was doing on myself cleared space for me to be me again. I could create new possibilities for myself, I had space to love again, space to create again, and space to be of service to anyone who needed me.

***

January, 2015. Seven months had passed. I was on the freeway and traffic was backed up for miles. I kept thinking that the cause might have been a bad accident, but as I got closer I saw that the freeway exit was blocked. I looked over and saw a man in a car with yellow tape surrounding it. I hoped that it wasn't my friend who washes cars at the gas station. When I got home and turned on the news, I saw that a police officer had shot and killed a young man. The next morning I got a call telling me that it was my cousin! I was numb because I was tired of all the police shootings all over this country, and now they killed one of mine. I was angry, sad, and hurt. My cousin's mom lost two of her other sons to the streets and now this. After my brother was murdered I joined an advocacy group in Oakland and had just met with the mayor of Oakland in January of 2015 to discuss the possibility of doing a community event to bring the community and police together to establish new relationships between them. I have friends on the police force that I had known for a long time, and once my cousin's name was released I got a text from Oakland's Mayor Libby Schaaf, and several officers that I knew called to send their personal condolences. This did not make me feel any better. Thank you, but my cousin is dead and now we have to go through the pain of burying him. Now not only was I directly affected by black on black crime, but my relative was shot wrongfully by law enforcement (OPD).

The anger was about to consume me. I felt like I had to turn grief, anger, and pain into a positive so I created "The Artivist Movement Oakland". I had local artists and speakers come for a day of entertainment and empowerment. I was tired of marching, it didn't seem like it was getting us anywhere. Every time we marched or rallied, the anarchists came in, tore our city down, and blamed it on the blacks. I didn't want that. I wanted to create a safe environment for everyone to voice their concerns on injustice in our community by using their art and divine expressions. The event was a huge success; I had the support of so many people in

104

the community. I paid out of my own pocket for the event, and it was money well spent. I felt good that I could put on such a great event and give back to the city that raised me. I have been to a lot of places and seen a lot of faces, but there's nothing like Oakland, California. I've since become an advocate for my city, working behind the scenes changing policies in Oakland that will make life better for the next generation. My life now is about helping and empowering others who may feel stuck in life to be resilient. I found happiness in making a difference, and by helping others find happiness I learned that it's not just about you. Sometimes you have to get lost to be found, and something negative has to "die" in order for you to transform into something positive. In this journey, you might fall and sometimes feel defeated; make the choice to get back up, find your sweet spot, and live in it.

Through all of my trials and tribulations, my difficulties and vicissitudes, my daughter was watching me. That is why it is very important to show our children how to live and treat people. You are their first example in life. Through it all I was able to raise a leader and a role model. She graduated from Oakland School for the Arts High School and was named the Boys and Girls Club Youth of the Year. She received scholarships and was honored by Oakland's mayor and city council. She was also given a proclamation from the city of Oakland. I could not have asked for a better child. All that I had worked for, all that I had given up, was worth it. If I didn't do anything right in this life, I knew that I did right by my daughter in this journey, and now I'm who God purposed me to be, an unstoppable leader. My life was not always a straight and narrow road. I had to take some u-turns and go down some dark paths to become the woman and leader that I am today. God does not use perfect people for his purpose, sometimes he has to use the very people that are the least likely to get the job done. I feel he does this to show us just how unstoppable we are. My intent for writing this book was to share my story to help someone. Don't be afraid to tell your story. Everything we go through in life is not about us, it's about building character and learning from our mistakes so that we can help others that may be going through what you have already been through. Don't let anything stop you! BE UNSTOPPABLE!

Letting Go

I'm letting go, got to fly higher than an eagle
I'm letting go, got to reach out to my father
To let him know I'm letting it go

The past... he wasn't there for my talent shows
And every time I would wait
Or ask could I go on late, just hoping my father would be there
To see me sing. None through my career did I see him in the rear.
Looking so proud I would always say out loud.
I wish my daddy was here.

I'm letting go, got to fly higher than an eagle
I'm letting go, got to reach out to my father
To let him know I'm letting it go

The past...he wasn't there when I needed him,
To give me the blueprint on how
A man was supposed to be.
Going through my teenage years he
Was a stranger to me. I would
Always say out loud, I wish
My daddy was here.

I'm letting go, got to fly higher than an eagle
I'm letting go, got to reach out to my father
To let him know I'm letting it go

Now that I am grown I can make it on my own
God moved in and showed me alone all a father could be.
I never missed a meal; I never had to steal another day in my life,
When He came in my life now all I say is I'm glad my Father is
here!

VI
Mama Said

How many of us have heard our parents say, "You're going to miss me when I am gone."? I never thought I would be living that so soon in my life; I always pictured my mother and I growing old together since she was so young when she had me.

My mother always had good advice for me and I always valued my mother's opinion and what she thought. Before she died I wanted to know everything I could. I picked her brain a lot. She told me that God had shown her already that I was going to be even more successful than I had already been. This surprised me because it was a confirmation from God. My mother planted a seed in me before she left this earth. Nobody could ever trick me into thinking that I am nothing less than successful. Why? Because my mother blessed my life by planting a word seed into my life. *Luke 8:11 – This is the meaning of a parable: The seed is the word of God.*

I sang at Mingles, a venue in Oakland, before she died. It was my way of still feeling close to what we used to do before she was unable to walk and sit up on her own. I remember coming from the gig and crawling into bed with her. She said, "Stacy, I want you to use the gifts God gave you for good and not for evil, would you promise me that?" I said, "Yes, but why do you say that?" She said that all my life she knew that I was not only gifted, but that I had spiritual gifts that the devil could trick me into using for him, so she said for me to keep God first and seek His kingdom. *Matthew 6:33 – But seek first His kingdom and His righteousness, and all these things will be given to you as well.*

All my life she would tell me to keep my nose clean and to not accept any wooden nickels. I later would find out what that meant, too. My childhood friend that I hung out with was a little loud and sometimes we would get into a lot of trouble growing up. We continued to get ourselves into little situations that were sometimes potentially deadly. My mother never said anything about her until she had just six months left to live. She told me that she and I were going in two different directions in life, and that I needed to put that relationship in check. She said that friend was holding me back. I never realized that she was right. She told me that you can dress a pig up, make it smell good, but when it's all said and done that pig is still going to wallow back in the mud, and that's just what happened. When you constantly involve yourself with people whose energy is not in alignment with yours, you will never move forward; that person and you become one. Birds of a feather flock together.

My mother told me that I would outgrow my daughter's father; she could not pay me to believe that in 1998. She was right, though. She also told me without a plan, then plan to fail. That is why I keep a Plan A, B, C, D and sometimes E.

My daughter Jaelyn was a year old when my mother passed, and she always told me that she was going to be a big girl for her age, and that I would always have to remind her of how old she is. Today Jaelyn is 17 and could pass for a 20 year old, not because she is fast, she's just very mature for her age.

When our parents say things to us, they're not trying to see us fail, they are trying to help. They have been where we are going. I do believe that with each generation we are little wiser than they were, but for they were put here to be our guide until we know God for ourselves, and then He becomes our guide. It's like we are in a dark forest and He is leading us, and then we think we see our way and move from His light that is shining to get us through the forest. That's when we find ourselves in darkness, associating with people we have no business being around. We get caught up in drugs and everything that the devil has in his darkness. God never stops shining that light, we have to find Him and the light so that we can move in the direction that God wants us to move in. If we seek Him first and His kingdom, everything else will be added. It's simple, but we make it difficult.

Now that I am a mother, I fully understand the frustration of a mother who is just trying to shield her child from getting hurt. One thing I realized is that even with me, my mother tried to shield me from trouble, but I still found it every time. The mistakes I made I had to go through to make me the person I am today.

As parents we cannot shield our children from everything. All we can do is guide them to the best of our ability. Keep them in the knowledge of God, teach them God's way at an early age so that when they become adults they won't stray too far from the way they were raised. (Deuteronomy 11:19) As a parent all you can do is your best, they have to walk their own path once they become adults. If you know that you did your best, there is nothing to worry about. Pray for your children and God will see them through. I know my mother prayed for me. I was headed to hell in a row boat, but one day God sent me through a humbling experience. I became a mother and lost my mother within a year, two life changing experiences at one time. It was more than enough to deal with, on top of not being spiritually stable or grounded. That is why it is important to stay spiritually grounded and anchored in the Lord (Hebrews 6:19), firm and secure.

When my daughter was born and I became a parent, everything my mother said to me started making more sense. I thought I knew it all when really I didn't. Life has a way of teaching us the hard way when we don't take heed to what our parents try to teach us. We set ourselves up for the greater lesson in life. When I was five months pregnant, my mother said to me "I don't know what kind of mother you're going to be!" I was so hurt, I couldn't understand why she would say that. Later on I realized the life I was living then was on the edge, and those words stuck to me when she passed, and because of it I made sure that I was the best damn mother to my child based on those words that penetrated me when she said them. My daughter is an adult child now and she and I have had our ups and downs but I never gave up on her. I was amazed that I raised such a well spoken, awesome daughter. I wish that Mama was here to see what type of parent I turned out to be.

My mother is not with me in the flesh, but she still lives on in my heart, and if I could have her back today in a healthy body I would, but my mother died for a reason. I know it sounds harsh, but it's true. I know now why she had to go. Instead of letting her death be the death of me, I let it become my life! I now celebrate her death day and mourn, and on her birthday I think of all the good memories I have of her.

Mom was so upset that she was not leaving a big fortune for my sister, brother, and me. I urged her not to feel that way because whether she knew it or not, she was leaving us rich! Rich spiritually, rich with knowledge, rich with the moneymaking tools to survive. And for this, no money could ever, ever, ever take the place of her life. She didn't realize that she deposited so much wealth into my life that I didn't need an inheritance. She raised me to be unstoppable.

In these next few chapters, I will share with you the steps I took to becoming unstoppable. It was important to me that you read my story, and now I'm going to share my glory! How do I wake up every day happy? How do I get out of bed with a great attitude and gratitude for each day after all that I have been through? Keep reading!

VII
Easy Going

Failure. When looking back at my failures in life, I came to realize that they were not really failures. It was God showing me that I was doing things my way and not His way. I was doing things the way I thought in my human mind I should be doing, going where I wanted to go and not where He wanted me to go. *Matthews 4:19 - Come follow me and I will make you fishers of men. At once they left their nets and followed him.*

When we fail, we often feel defeated. If we consulted God on every end of our decision making, we will not fail. When we ask God for direction and advice, He will advise you according to His plan. God will never lead you astray when you include Him in your planning. *Isaiah 14:24 - the Lord almighty has sworn, surely, as I have planned, so it will be, and as I have purposed, so it will stand.*

When you feel that you have failed, just tell yourself it's a blessing in just recognizing that failure. Remember the old saying "If at first you don't succeed, dust yourself off and try again."

When I was losing my house to foreclosure, I felt like the world's biggest loser. I felt like I had failed myself and my daughter, but suddenly I realized that this too was a test from God to see how I would handle my circumstances. I began to applaud myself for trying, and if I tried I would never fail! Not every challenge that we face from day to day is a punishment from God. He does not work that way. Sometimes we pray for patience and God puts you in a situation that will challenge your patience. I was about to lose my condominium. I was so afraid of failure in my mind; if I lost my condo, I would be failing. But the only failing part would have been not stepping out when I had the chance to buy, not losing it.

Now that I have experience in becoming a homeowner, I am more knowledgeable about the home buying experience and the foreclosure processes. What a blessing!

***

Lack. Many times we experience a lack in many areas of our life we have attracted into our lives one way or another. In my case, it was both misappropriating money and not being a good steward over the money God allowed me to have. I was spending money on frivolous things, eating out every night, going to big department stores and spending top dollar for things that I knew I could not afford from high end clothes and shoes, etc. Think about it right now - what have you spent money on that was not in your budget?

I always made good money by singing and by being a hair stylist but I could never seem to keep any of the money I was making. I never saw a large savings account. Why? I had a need for lack of money; somehow, I did not feel that I deserved a large bank account. I was too busy spending my money as fast as I received it. I would never take out any percentage for my savings. I was not being a good steward over my money.

When we are blessed with money, the first thing we do is spend money on ourselves. I'm not saying that you should not treat yourself, I am simply saying that we are blessed to be a blessing to others. When we give out, we get back. Most of us are lacking not only financially but spiritually as well because we do not give to others. Release the thought of lack. It is so much better to give than receive. I found that making someone happy is more powerful than you can possibly imagine. Studies have shown that giving will put a much bigger smile on your face than spending on yourself. Enriching the lives of others makes us all wealthier. True wealth is not about your earthly possessions, but by leading a fulfilled life, and knowing you've made a difference in someone's life.

I was in a financial dry spot at one time in my life. I was drowning in debt and didn't know where my next meal was going to come from. Yet somehow I still had the heart to give. As scared as I was, I knew that if I helped somebody doing worse than me even in my dry spot, God would see my heart and bless my efforts. And He did.

Temptation. When I began using drugs, I was overcome by trouble and sorrow. I was on the devil's playground. I was teeter tottering with death, and if anybody knows the devil's purpose, you know that he came to kill and destroy. *John 10:10 - His interest is in himself not you. When I turned to God and confessed my sin and cried out for God to save me, He did. He gave me rest beyond rest, peace. He picked me up out of darkness and placed me in the light. God is an ever present help in the time of trouble.* God does not tempt us, temptation is directly from the devil. I grew up in West Oakland and East Oakland, surrounded by dope fiends all of my life. I never wanted to know how they got to that point in their lives. The devil put drugs on a silver platter to attempt to trick me. I was doing drugs in mansions under the Hollywood sign, I was with the who's who of Hollywood and top celebrities. The devil made it seem like I was on top of the world, that I was better than anyone else, but in reality I was no better than the dope fiends that were on the streets of Oakland. You have to be careful because the devil will make it seem like it's the best thing ever, when really it's a set-up, a trap for death! The enemy is tricky, and he will not stop until he robs, steals, or kills you!

***

Waiting. Sometimes in life we want things now, we don't want to wait for anything. But God has His way of teaching us patience through waiting. Sometimes we are not ready for the things that we want. God has to work on us in order to be able to handle the blessings and the things we desire.

I would always wonder why, when I've worked with some of the best rappers and singers in the music industry, I hadn't made it to the point of being noticed on a major scale. Not until recently was it revealed to me that I was not yet ready mentally. If I was famous back when I was dealing with my addictions and self-destruction, I would be in the tabloids as much as Paris Hilton, Brittney Spears, and Nicole Richie all put together. God did not see that for me. He wanted me to be spiritually mature before dealing with being famous and among the recognized. Everyone has a time to shine, be thankful for where you are right now. Be patient and you will get whatever you're waiting for when the time is right. Be patient and stay focused on your vision.

**

Illness. I believe we create every so-called illness in our own bodies. The body is a mirror of our inner thoughts and beliefs. Every cell within your body responds to every single thought you think and every word you speak. Continuous modes of thinking and speaking negatively produces diseases.

Often there are times when someone is diagnosed with cancer and the doctor suggests that they immediately do surgery. No. First, fix the root of the problem. The problem is not the cancer, it's the thought patterns that caused the cancer in the first place. Have you ever wondered why when someone goes into surgery to get the cancer removed and it spreads like wildflowers? You have to first work on the inside before you fix the outside; otherwise, the problem is still there. Start your healing from the inside out. Anger, anxiety, depression, and resentment are all illness breeders. To protect yourself, identify and address your feelings before you lose control. Studies show that when you get angry it causes a dip in the antibody immunoglobulin A levels, which in turn break down your ability to fight infection. Deal with your core issues and live a healthy life.

**

Disappointments. You can never give with the intention of receiving. Never do something expecting something in return. We allow ourselves to be disappointed. The definition of disappointment is "the feeling of being let down: a feeling of sadness or frustration because something was not as good, attractive, or satisfactory as expected or because something hoped for did not happen." I have been disappointed more than I care to mention; I have been disappointed by my father, friends, and family. What I learned is that I cannot put trust in man; man will fail you every time, but God will go all the way with you. He will not leave you. *Deuteronomy 31:6 – Be strong and courageous. Do not be afraid or terrified because of them, for the Lord your God* *goes with you; he will never forsake you. Romans 5:5 – And hope does not put us to shame, because God's love has been poured out into our hearts through the Holy Spirit, who has been given to us.*

***

Relationships. People come into our lives for a reason and a season. However, everyone who comes into your life is not God sent. There are people who come into your life from day one who deplete you in every way spiritually, physically, and financially. These are the people who are sent from a negative force or directly from the devil. These people are sent into your life as a distraction. They are around to distract you from your purpose and mission. People who are sent by God enhance who you are; they are people who help you connect the divine dots in your life. You will know exactly who they are because you will feel that they are God sent. It will be a spiritual connection.

The truth is the truth; you know what is real by the way you feel. There is no in-between. We often see the signs but choose to not to look at it for what it is. That is where we make our mistakes.

I was in a relationship with a man that I had known for 22 years. I was comfortable with him, and I thought he was the one for me. God sent me signs that I did not pay attention to, and I remained in this on and off relationship for two years hoping things would change. Two years later, I was going through the same thing. After bumping my head a second time, I finally realized that he and I were going in two different directions. I was fooling myself if I believed that he was the man God sent for me. It was not God's will for me to be with this man. I kept trying to make it work and God said no. How many times was I going to keep bumping my head in this relationship?

Relationships are mirrors of ourselves. What we attract always mirrors either qualities we have or beliefs we have about relationships. It could be a boss, a co-worker, friend, lover, or child. The things you don't like about these people are either what you yourself do or what you believe in. You can't attract these people in your life if the way they are didn't complement or mirror you in some way.

117

Let's say you have a friend who is unreliable and lets you down. Look within. Where in your life are you unreliable, and when do you let others down? Look at your own life for a moment.

Think of someone in your life right now that bothers you. Describe three things about this person that you don't like. Now look deeply inside of you and ask yourself "How am I like that?" Give your self some time. Now ask yourself if you are willing to change that within yourself.

Grief. *How to get up the day after.* It may sound crazy, but you have to thank God and go into praise and worship mode. You have to thank Him first for waking you up to see another day and ask Him to show you your purpose since you were the one left here on earth. When our loved ones transition into the spirit world, they pass the baton to those of us still living. This means that you are the one that will finish the race, and when you leave you pass the baton to the living to keep the family legacy alive. Each and every day I wake up, I stand on the shoulders of my mother, father, brother, and maternal grandparents as well as all of my cousins that have passed. I get up and go on knowing that they are on the sidelines cheering me on. They give me strength to get up the next day and make things happen. I have good days and bad days, but overall this way of living in sorrow, misery, sadness, anguish, pain, distress, heartache, heartbreak, agony, torment, and affliction does not serve you. It will not allow you to live life to its full potential, so wake up every day knowing that your loved one wants you to continue life and live abundantly.

How to cope with sudden changes in your lifestyle. The sudden death of a loved one can change the survivor's lives forever. When my mother passed I had six months to prepare for her death. With my brother and my father, their deaths were so sudden that there was no time to prepare. The difficulty with sudden death is that it is unforeseeable and often involves car accidents, gun violence, heart attacks, strokes, or suicide. Sudden death is most times hardest on the family because there is no time to say goodbye. The recovery is complicated. With my brother, I chose to take his music and continue our music project by any means necessary. I start-

118

ed looking at it as he passed me the baton to carry out what we started, and it gave me strength to cope. When my father passed, I had to move in to take care of my grandmother because he helped take care of her. When he passed suddenly, we had to make some sudden changes; I moved in to take care of my grandmother; I did it with no complaints, and it actually helped me cope with the loss of my father. Being able to to be present to help my grandmother gave me great joy.

How to live without your loved one. You will never "get over it." You just learn to live without them. I was used to my brother calling and coming by my house every day, sometimes three times a day to eat, etc. The next day after the funeral is "wake up call day" as I call it. When no one calls or comes by, it's the worst feeling ever. The next day after my brother's funeral, I woke up and I went to my front door, opened it, went on the porch and literally looked down the street to see if he was going to come down the street. I had a panic attack; my mind still had not processed the fact that he was gone. As the months went by, I got better. What I realized is that our loved ones are not in human bodies, but their spirits live on. We miss them physically because we can't see them, but if you pay attention, they will let you know they are right there with you. At first I was afraid when I felt the presence of my loved ones who have passed, but over the years I have learned how to embrace and enjoy these moments. In reality they are still with us, just not in a physical body.

The hardest things for me over the years was birthdays, the anniversary of the day of death, and the holidays. On my mother's birthday, May 21, I would spend in bed in tears. The next month, June 16th, was the anniversary of her death. These were two months out of the year that I knew I would be depressed. My brother and father passed in September, which was also my birthday month. I could not continue to be depressed on these significant days and I eventually turned it around. On May 21, I released my first single on iTunes, and on June 16th I began to celebrate Tupac's birthday. September 12th was the day my brother was murdered, and I turned that day around by celebrating my good friend's birthday. I turned what was a sad day into a great day! On these days that once made me sad, I now make those days matter, and I enjoy life.

How to ensure your loved one's death will not be in vain. When my mother died I promised that I would take better care of my health and help others to become aware of good eating habits and overall live healthier lives. My father died of a heart attack and stroke. My father did not die in vain. I now have a diet that does not include fried artery clogging foods. I owe having a healthier diet to my father and mother. My brother was murdered by gun violence. Although I cannot stop gun violence, I am now pro-peace, pro-love, and compassionate. I am very active in my community, involving myself in being a part of the solution. I stand on the shoulders of all of my loved ones who are gone to ensure that their deaths are not in vain.

Find others who can truly say, "I understand what you're going through." When my mother died, I did not go to any support groups; I felt like I didn't need to. But if you asked my friends who were not going through what I was going through, they would have told you, "Yes, she needs to go." I kept talking to people who had no point of reference of what I was feeling; they didn't know the pain because they had their parents and siblings. When my brother was murdered, it actually took the life out of me; I was numb for so long, I finally joined a advocacy group called 'Their Lives Matter", a group of women and men who had lost sons, daughters, sisters, brothers, and husbands in Oakland due to gun violence. It was refreshing to be around people who could truly understand how I felt. It's important to surround yourself with support groups, or people who have gone through what you're going through for moral support. You cannot do this alone, you need spiritual guidance along with support from others who understand what you're going through.

Create a memorable legacy for your loved one. My mother passed in 2000, and by 2004 I was ready to create a memorable legacy in mother's name by starting the Sharon Randolph Founda-

120

tion, helping women fighting cancer look and feel good. You may not want to start a foundation in your loved one's memory, but there are many things you can do to honor them and create a legacy. You can start your own support group, you can create a scholarship fund. Get creative! Your loved ones are still rooting for you in the spirit world.

How to turn your pain and hurt into help for others. TELL YOUR STORY! We all have been through some type of hurt and or pain. The difference between my story and yours is that I'm telling mine and you're not. There is nothing that we go through on this earth that we face alone. There are people who are out there hurting just like you are. I am a firm believer that what we go through, we go through to help someone else along the way. This way we have credibility when we step out to help. No one wants to get help from someone who has never been through anything. It can be addictions, or it can be loss of a loved one or spouse. For me, it was the pain of loss. Writing this book and recording the soundtrack to this book motivated me to turn pain into help for others. I love you that much that I shared the good, the bad, and the ugly of my life to reach out to someone who may be going through what I have already been through. For you it may not be a book; whatever you're going through, please know that you're going to help someone with the same struggle some day. Do not be afraid to share with others; helping others is helping yourself too.

Today is a Good Day

I have my health and strength, I have
Legs to get out of bed with, I have hands to brush
My teeth and wash my face.

I have a loving living space.
I am grateful for all these things
And more, before I walk out the door.

Today is a good day!

How are you today?
I can't complain, if so who would
Listen anyway? Mortgage due, bills due
And still I smile knowing
God will save me, I am His child.
Can't dwell on yesterday, I gotta stay focused on moving ahead.

Today is a good day!
Today I am a magnet to success
I am a magnet to the people who need me
I am a magnet to wealth and prosperity
I am a magnet to riches. I am
A magnet to the publicity I need.

Today is a good day!

VIII
Ridiculous Blessings

I was told that sticks and stones will hurt your bones but words would never hurt me. When my daughter started school and the kids said mean things to her, I told her the same thing but I realize now that words do hurt. It's up to you, though, whether or not you're going to put value in what someone says about you, good or bad. One thing that I do know is that being misunderstood hurts.

When we are not secure in ourselves, we often place value in what other people think of us. The very same person who told you that you were beautiful might be the same person who tells you that you are ugly. As long as *you* feel that you are beautiful, it doesn't matter what anyone else thinks.

When we learn self-confidence and confidence in the Holy Spirit, you'll find that He is the truth and the light. We can always count on people being people; we all are human.

***

The Four Signs of Hurt

Hardened heart. When you harden your heart you close up and don't trust anyone because you have held in the hurt from past relationships and circumstances. We tend to hide behind things such as sex, food, and addictions when we're hurting. Your heart becomes a heart of stone. When we truly forgive people who have done us wrong, it allows God to work in our lives and renew our hearts. *Ezekiel 36:26-27 - I will give you a new heart and put a spirit in you; I will remove from you your heart of stone and give you a heart of flesh. And I will put my Spirit in you and move you to follow my decrees and be careful to keep my laws.*

Pretending that you don't hurt. We often walk around and pretend that nothing is bothering us, and we go about our life like we are OK. We must learn to deal with our hurt and face it.

123

There is nothing wrong with hurting; we are human and circumstances that we experience in life will often cause pain. When Lazarus died the Bible says Jesus wept. (John 11:35) If Jesus could weep who are we? It's OK to cry and feel hurt, just do not drown yourself in it. Especially for men; it's OK to cry.

Most men when they are young are taught that boys don't cry, and they grow up feeling like they're soft if they show emotions. We are all human, and we all have feelings. Address those feelings and move past the anger and frustration.

Deciding not to trust. When we base our new relationships on what we have endured in past relationships, it simply means that you have not released the old circumstances, and you carry it into the next relationship.

We have to realize that until you heal from the past you cannot move forward. Simply running away from the problem will cause you to meet that same problem and person until you completely heal and choose to trust again. That person that hurt you ten years ago is still in your consciousness because you choose not to ever trust another woman or man again based on what someone did to you ten years ago. It's not fair to the new person and relationship that your creating for yourself. Your past will continue to be in your future until you release it.

Unforgiving heart. When we do not forgive, we hold an account of someone's wrongdoings. Do you know where we would be if God held an account of all of our wrongdoings? I don't want to think about it. We as believers have no time to hold an account on wrongdoings because we know that we are not perfect and we will make mistakes that one day will require someone to forgive us.

***

Making your own choices

Do you look for others to give you solutions? Do you make decisions based on what someone else said you should do? Do you call your sister, mother, best friend, or family member whenever something goes wrong?

I always called my mother to help me make decisions. When my mother died, I had to turn to God. It was a most humbling experience for me. I had to rely on God to see me through. For the first time in my life the saying, "God will be a mother" became a reality. *Proverbs 3:5-6 – Trust in the Lord with all your heart and lean not on your own understanding. In all your ways submit to Him and He will make your paths straight.*

Life is unpredictable and we'll never know when our safe person or problem solver may not be there for us. The next time you are faced with a problem, don't pick up the phone. Write down the solutions and you'll get your own problem worked out. If you are still confused, get on your knees, meditate, and pray. God is a problem solver, try Him. You have to be willing to be still and wait for Him to answer you. *Psalms 46:10 – He says, "Be still, and know that I am God; I will be exalted among the nations, I will be exalted in the earth."*

When I had the opportunity to purchase my property, there were so many people telling me not to buy at that time. I started thinking, "No, I'll wait until next year when I have a little more money." I woke up one day and told myself I was going to step out on faith. I was scared, but I did it. I went out, got my pre-approval letter, looked for a place, and put in an offer on the ideal place for me. It had three bedrooms plus a loft, and was ideal for me for running my business from home. I did not have the closing costs but I stepped out on faith. My closing costs were $8,000 and I wrote the check like the money was there. I said, "God, if this is for me, the check will clear. If not, I will be still." That next day I got a call from my Realtor saying that the seller was going to pay $5,000 of my closing cost, leaving me with only $3,000 to come up with. That same day a client of mine called me and asked me if he could pay for his services and products for the whole year. It was unbelievable. I acted on faith. God moved on my behalf and it was only because I stepped out on faith and moved with faith. Faith is nothing without work. You have to put action behind your faith. We serve a God we cannot see, which means we have to act before we can see the outcome. How can we say that we trust God without faith? We can't, so let go and let God. *Luke 17:6 - He*

125

replied, "If you have faith as small as a mustard seed, you can say to this mulberry tree, 'Be uprooted and planted in the sea,' and it will obey you."

If I had continued to rent I would have never come to the point in my life where I had to reinvent myself or my business. I would have been content with paying $1,300 a month rent and clearing two sales per month at $4,000. No. Instead what happened was that I was brought to another level because my monthly expenses were greater. I was forced to reinvent by business so that I could reach the next level. If I would have listened to others, I would still have a small business mentality, renting and never becoming a homeowner.

Listen to that small still voice in your head; most times it's the voice that says jump off of this ledge and take a chance. When it's God's voice, you can jump and He will catch you every time.

IX
Old Junk, Let It Go

Have you ever let trash pile up on your lawn or in front of your house? Most likely you would pay someone to keep the lawn manicured and clean or do it yourself. If not, the trash would pile up and you would most likely have angry neighbors because your house makes the community look bad. Instead you pick up the trash as it blows onto your lawn or else it would take more time and money to clean it otherwise. It's the same for junk or trash in our lives. We have to be willing to get rid of all the trash that has blown into our lives when it comes whatever the circumstance is, whether it's a break up, holding resentment, blame, or unforgiveness. If we don't clear the trash in our lives as it comes, the circumstances will pile up and weigh us down to the point that we don't prosper. We become embedded with trash in our lives, and it becomes a reflection of our lives as well.

Steps Toward Letting It Go

Forgiveness. True forgiveness is not holding an account of someone's wrongdoings. Forgive and let it go. When someone asks you for forgiveness, forgive them. (Luke 17:3) Forgive them even if they don't ask for forgiveness. Forgiveness is for you, not the other person. When you forgive, you release the other person from your cosmic storage; they no longer take up space in your mind. Most times when someone does something wrong to us, we don't forgive them because they didn't acknowledge the wrong they did to us. Most times we talk to people that have nothing to do with the situation and the person never even knows that you're upset. Go to the person that offended or hurt you and let them know how it impacted your life.

Forgiveness is also being thankful for that experience you had with the person. A year after my mother died, a good friend of mine slept with my daughter's father and it hurt me. I forgave her and I was so thankful for the experience because she showed me who she was. Maya Angelo said, "When someone shows you who they are, believe them." I needed to see that she was not someone whom I could trust. The moment I forgave her in my heart, I released her. Take the positive approach to every situation. It is a blessing in knowing, and whether you perceive it to be good or bad, there is a lesson to learned from it.

When I was replaced in the group Image I had to forgive the ladies quickly. I remember calling them and squashing the feud because at the end of the day, I really wanted them to succeed. As a result of moving forward and not holding back forgiveness, I was able to do their hair for Vibe Magazine which gave me print credits that I would need as a freelance hair artist. You block yourself when you don't forgive. If I hadn't forgiven them, I would have missed the opportunity to display my other talent within the group, which was doing hair.

In 2009 when my brother was murdered, I went through several emotions: anger, blame, sadness, revenge, hurt, you name it. I finally came to a place where I could forgive the individual who killed my brother. I prayed the next day and asked God to cover the young man who killed my brother. I asked God to protect him long enough to make it to jail, and I asked God to not let him get the death penalty either. I wanted him to live long enough to get his life right with God so that he could see my brother in God's kingdom. A year later the homicide detective called me and my sister and asked us to to come to his office. He told us that the young man had been picked up. Later he was sentenced to 200 years in prison! I knew at that point that it worked out in my favor. I wanted more than revenge for this young man. I wanted him to see God one day, I wanted him to live and not die. It was not about an eye for an eye with me, it was about his eternal life.

Forgiving exercise. Take out a sheet of paper. Think about the person that you need to forgive, and think about how life would be if you were not bitter towards them. What would life be like? What would you be doing with that person? How would you feel if that were possible?

Release resentment. We often experience resentment

towards others when we find it hard to forgive them. Resentment, criticism, guilt, anger, and bitterness are considered to be components of deep hurt. We may feel we've been treated unfairly or wronged and we let the resentment live inside of us, feeding our negative emotions. If this is not dealt with or goes unresolved, the resentment fuels anger. This is unhealthy, and the long-term effect on doing so is illness. Cancer and other terminal illnesses can be caused by this way of being. These are all thoughts that poison the body.

I had deep resentment. By the time I was in my 30's I was still angry about my mother dying. I had not forgiven myself for past mistakes, and I still had a little resentment towards my father even though I thought I had forgiven him. There were three main things that I worked on to release this emotion:

Express yourself. When someone hurts us whether intentionally or accidentally, we have the right to express to that person the pain they caused and how it affected our lives. When I began expressing my feelings and not holding the pain in, I began to feel better inside. I would often be in a situation where I would be mad at someone and everyone else knew that I was mad at that person. I would never tell the person to whom it mattered. Go to them directly and express how you feel.

Communicate your feelings. Choose the right words to effectively communicate how you feel. Often times we will get mad at someone and choose not to say what is bothering us. Effectively communicating your feelings is good for you and the other person. You are telling them how you feel, and now they are aware of how you feel and can make the necessary adjustments to honor your feelings, or not. Either way it's a winning situation; they know how you feel. Your feelings matter even when you think they don't.

Practice forgiving. When we choose to forgive, sometimes the ill feelings creep back in from time to time. When that happens, say to yourself, "I have forgiven this person and I have no room for bitterness to take place in my life." Repeat this as many times as you need to as a reminder and an affirmation at the same time.

Remember, forgiveness is for you, it sets you free from resentment. When you embrace forgiveness, resentment will no longer have power over you or your life. You can release resentment by simply saying to yourself, "I lovingly forgive and release all of my past hurts. I choose to fill my world with joy. I love and approve of myself." It's that easy.

Release Blame. The hardest person to forgive was my father. He never told me I was beautiful or hugged me. I blamed him for all of my failed relationships, and I really felt in my heart that my dad didn't love me. I finally decided that I wanted to make a change in my life and grow. I had to learn to forgive my father; the hurt and resentment was weighing me down. I turned it around with a more positive perception of my father. I realized that he was not to blame for any of my past failed relationships. I also realized that I was independent because I was independent; none of that was my father's fault.

My mother was given six months to live and I purposely paid attention to how my father interacted with his immediate family. I found that none of them hugged each other, not even my grandmother. I never saw him embrace his father, mother, or siblings. How was my father supposed to give me something he did not receive himself? He could not give me what he never had been taught. Embracing each other and saying 'I love you' was not what he was taught. It caused me to look deeper. I actually felt empathy for him; after that I began to shower him, my grandparents, and uncles with love and hugs. I changed my perception and saw something totally different by releasing blame.

When we blame others and do not take responsibility for our own actions, we give away our power. There are times in life when we blame our parents or someone else for the circumstances in our life today. When you stop blaming others you will see the good in that situation or circumstance. Blaming others does not help you to look within. Whatever happened in your childhood was then and this is now; start living in the now. Why? Because if you live in the now you will be totally focused on where you're going and not where you've been.

Forgive yourself. Find a way to forgive yourself. God said if we confess our sins and ask for forgiveness, He will forgive us. If God has forgiven you, why not forgive yourself? There is no reason to condemn yourself and live in condemnation. That is why we are to forgive others because when we need to be forgiven, we want God to have mercy on us, and He will.

_I Am..._

I am free and safe in knowing that the maker
Of the universe knows what's best for me
And though I go through struggles, I sleep at night
Worry free.

I am I know that I am
Safe within His arms
I am and I know that I am
Major, favored in His eyes.

I am perfect, I am peace
I love, I am devoted
I am prosperous, I am a creator
I am a songwriter, I am a parent
I am a singer, I am an entrepreneur
I am a leader.

I am, I know that I am
Safe within His arms
I am and I know that I am
Major, favored in His eyes.

X
Unstoppable

Step out of the vicious circle. In 1997, there was a hit comedy movie *How To Be a Player* starring Bill Belamy. I recorded a song with Ant Banks that Def Jam pulled for the movie score. I went to the theater to see the movie, and as I'm watching it, all of sudden the actor says, "Shh! Y'all be quiet! Here comes the hook!" and to my surprise it was me singing the hook to the song. I sat in the movie theater on the verge of tears! I could not believe it; my voice was in this movie and I was not getting paid one dollar. For years I blamed Ant Banks for not telling me that he submitted the song for the movie when in reality he never submitted the song at all. Def Jam pulled the song from Jive Records for the soundtrack and movie score. It took me years to let go of feeling like I was cheated, when in reality I was not. I was work-for-hire and I got paid for the song, that was it. It is a human tendency to combine what happened with "the story" about what really occurred. When we do this, it is is hard to separate the two. What happened is Def Jam pulled the song for the movie. The story I created was that he submitted the song without telling me, which was so far from the truth. Have you ever called someone that didn't pick up, and right then and there you create a story as to why they didn't answer? There is 'what actually happened' and then there is a 'story about what happened'. Focus on the facts and not the story; the story most times does not support the facts. When I discovered this tendency and began to decipher between what really happened versus my story, I began to experience more joy and effectiveness.

Help others. What can you do to help others? Our constant mission in life should be to make ourselves available to help others, in every way possible. God works through people and if we allow Him to work through us, we are working within His will and purpose. A lot of times we get caught up in our day to day routines and we don't think about anyone but ourselves; sometimes you have to look outside of yourself to help others. When you help someone you are helping yourself. If we see someone stumble, we are not to become happy or rejoice in someone's failures. We are to uplift them and help them. You know where you've been but you don't know where you're going in your journey. You never know when you will need help after stumbling in your own journey. *Ecclesiastes 4:10 – If either of them falls down, one can help the other up. But pity anyone who falls and has no one to help them up.*

I remember a man standing on the corner. He asked me for money, I said no and kept walking. Something in me made me go back to the young man and give him words of encouragement. He explained to me that he was an injured vet and that he was waiting on an appeal to receive his VA benefits. I was so upset I didn't have a dime to give him that tears came to eyes. I didn't have any money and I was going through my own issues, but I had a smile and encouraging words for him. He wiped my eyes and said, "Don't cry, you have just given me more than money! You lifted me up. Thank you!" You may not always have money to give, but you can give the best gift ever and that's a smile, a hello, or a hug. We all need love and compassion, and it doesn't cost you anything to smile, or give someone encouraging words. I smile at everyone, even if they don't smile back. Often times you never know what people are going through.

***

Be honest and sincere with yourself and others

Forcing yourself to things you don't like. Has someone ever asked you to do something that you didn't want to do but you did it anyway? Alternatively, have you ever asked someone to do something for you and they beat around the bush before they gave you a definitive answer? How did both situations make you feel?

In my early twenties, I was not very honest with others or myself. Many times my friends would ask me for favors that I really did not want to do. Instead of saying no I would say yes, then do it begrudgingly. That stemmed from me not being true to myself, and not wanting to hurt anyone's feelings. I didn't allow

134

my individuality and uniqueness to shine through. I was not being my true self, I conformed to the expectations of others. It takes courage to be true to you. It requires you to look into yourself, be bold, sincere, and open-minded.

I had a friend that had just broken up with her boyfriend. She felt so depleted, and the whole time she was with her boyfriend she kept saying that she felt so stupid; she had done a lot of things in the relationship that she did not want to do and now he was on to the next. Do not compromise who are for anyone. It is important to stand for something or you will fall for anything. Be true to yourself and others and you will notice that you feel better at the end of the day.

Be true to yourself. Be true to your own values, never be afraid to voice your opinion or let your voice be heard. Fitting in is the worst. You are not operating as your true authentic self. Most times we experience this in grade school and never really grow out of it, we just get older and become adults that try to fit in. Being your true self allows you to shine from the inside out. You choose whether or not you want to shine or put your light out to please others. I used to dummy myself down so that other women wouldn't feel insecure by my presence. I stopped doing that when I realized that I was not being my true authentic self. Why should I put my light out to please others? Now when I walk into a room and command the attention of those in the room, I embrace it! I am who I am, and I will not dim my light for others. So to you my readers, please do not dim your light. Be your true self at all times.

***

Be good at finding the positive aspect in every obstacle. Every challenge that we face from day to day is not a punishment from God, He does not work that way. Sometimes we pray for patience and God puts you in a situation that will challenge that patience.

We have to look at life through our spiritual eyes, and our spiritual eyes are just that. We cannot see a spirit or touch one. The same thing applies to our challenges and trials. We can't see them coming nor can we touch them, but if we learn something from

135

them and see the good in every situation when they do reach our lives, we will look at challenges in a whole new light.

When my mother passed I could not see the silver lining in the fact that my mother died at 46 years old. As years began to pass, I realized that my mother would not have been able to take my brother's death, and it dawned on me that God had to take her before he took him. In addition, I was so happy that my mother was not alive to witness her baby being violently taken away from her.

When I had to solely rely on a bike for transportation, I would say, "Thank God I don't have to pay for parking and gas." It was true, I was saving so much money riding my bike. I chose to look at this way so that I would not fall into depression from not having a car.

***

Become more optimistic every day. It is important to become optimistic in every way; at home, school, work, and church. Every morning that you wake up, you should expect the best out of each day. Affirm to yourself that today is a good day, tell yourself that you are beautiful even when you're not feeling that way.

Let's say that you're late for work one day and you take the wrong exit while speeding off the freeway. Most times we cause ourselves to go into a big panic about getting to work on time. Instead, think of it this way: maybe God was saving you from a car accident on the exit that you normally take in the mornings. There are no mistakes; one concept to knowing that you are in control is knowing that you have no control.

After my foreclosure in 2007, my daughter and I went into the leasing office of an apartment home to apply for a town home. My daughter saw the look on my face when the lady came back and said we were not approved. As soon as we got to the car she said, "Mommy, it's OK. God has something better for us. Who knows, this place might make us sick or the plumbing might be bad. Who knows?" That was the most encouraging thing I had heard all day, and coming from a nine year old it was amazing. My daughter had been listening to me and gave my advice right back to me. I am a firm believer in what is for you will not pass you. If you believe that passage, you will never feel slighted, or like you missed an opportunity.

***

Love being alive. There was a point in my life when I did not love being alive. I woke up every day almost wishing something would happen to me so that I could be with my immediate relatives that had passed. I had no zeal for life. What was life without my mother, being here with me to encourage me, and tell me how proud she was of me? What was life without my father being the life of the party? What was life without my brother being here to get on my nerves, and make music with?

***

Practice Positive Meditation

- Imagine how your success will make you feel.

- Allow the images of success to become clear.

- Hold the images of success in your mind for long periods.

- Enjoy making the images in your mind become reality.

Positive affirmations to say to yourself

- I am a goal achiever, through and through.

- When I commit to something, I stick with it.

- I keep focused on the benefits of reaching my goals.

- Benefits are what compel me and drive me toward my goals.

- I expect and expect abundance to flow easily to me.

- I am a co–creator with God.

***

Release the procrastinating attitude. We come up with hundreds of reasons why the time is not right; we often end up saying, "This isn't the right time." Most likely if you're a procrastinator you'll say things like "I'll do it tomorrow" or "I'll call tomorrow." Why put off until tomorrow what you can do today?

***

Release the fear of failure. Take a minute to think about what would happen in your life if you were not afraid to fail?

What would be different about your life right now, if you had done those things that you were afraid to do? We all have been afraid that if we try something new we might fail. My mother would always say "Nothing beats a fail but a try."

I had a client who asked me to make a full hair piece out of four old hair pieces that he had bought over the years. I actually laughed at him and told him it was impossible. He said, "Stacy, I had a vision that we could do this." I said to him, "Let's do it!" As long as there is a vision, you can make it happen. If we tried and failed, we really didn't fail because we tried. I actually surprised myself. I made his vision a reality. I had to give myself a pat on the back for that one. The fear in this situation was the unknown; I had never taken four hairpieces and made one whole unit, so because I had never done it I said it could not be done. Do not let anyone tell you what can't be done. If you can see it, you can achieve it and make it manifest.

When I went to Japan for three months, I went with $100 in my pocket. If I would have been afraid to step out, I would have never known that I could survive in another country doing what I loved to do - my divine expression, singing. Just by moving in faith and believing that I would make it, I ended up getting a job singing and had money to live off of and send home. I did not let fear hold me back. If I would have stayed home on the "Ifs", I would be still wondering today what it would be like if I had gone to Japan. There is nothing to fear but fear itself. Here are a few steps to assist you in walking by faith:

138

Believe it's already yours. You have to believe that whatever you ask for has already been given to you. It's called receiving. You cannot receive anything from someone without first reaching for it and opening your hands to receive it. Try reaching out to get something with your hands closed. You can't do it, right? The same thing applies to the things we ask from God; we don't have it because we are not reaching out with an open hand; you have to mentally receive it by believing. When we pray and ask God for anything, we must believe it is already done. This is another level of faith that we have to come to be in tune with. We can't pray and ask God for something and then as soon as you finish your prayer, you are stressing over that situation. You have to believe that the car you just prayed for is in your garage or outside your home; you've got to believe that husband that you prayed for is walking around this earth looking for you.

Walk in crazy faith. When I decided to write this book I had no idea how to structure it. I just knew that God said for me to do it and I followed. I wrote from my heart, day after day, until it became what you are reading today. I also knew that there were people out there that needed to hear what I had to say about how I began healing my life. I knew that I was not alone and that I could help somebody with my testimony. I didn't have a writing degree or a PhD, but I took action and started writing. I didn't let fear stop me. I had never written a book, but I did it anyway. When God gives you a vision, act on it and do it. First you have to understand your potential. It's all attitude; the more you practice the attitude of achievement, the more certain you'll become. I can do all things through Christ who strengthens me. (Philippians 4:13) No matter what, God will equip you with the tools you need to complete your task for Him.

Whatever you wish to achieve in your life, you must get to the point where you believe in yourself, always. It doesn't matter if anyone tells you it is not possible, or that you can't. Always know that you can, you are, and you will *achieve.*

Be willing to take action. Taking action will help you to move forward with no excuses. What steps do you need to take to put your plan into action? What can you do to start making your

139

dreams become a reality? Do it. Remember to surround yourself with positive people who think like you, otherwise you will be surrounded with people who are holding you back. Their energy will hold you down. Surround yourself with people who uplift you and help you to reach your goals, then sit back and watch yourself soar like an eagle.

Put a time line on your goals. This will help you to stay focused. When you put a time line on your goals you will begin taking action in your life to move toward your goals. Nothing can happen without forward movement. Begin by being more positive. Treat people differently. When you're supportive of others, you will get back the same positive energy you put into others.

Be willing to take risks. Taking risks is one of the first things that I learned while becoming an entrepreneur. Yes, it was scary at first but when I stepped out and succeeded, it made me want to take more risks. I don't mean risks like going to Las Vegas and gambling your life savings away; I'm talking about business risks.

I opened my first hair salon at age 21. I was so afraid because I had the "what if" syndrome. What if no one comes to me? How am I going to get salon furniture? What if this is not the right neighborhood? All of those questions were pessimistic questions.

One day I just said to myself, "God did not bring me this far to leave me." I put it in His hands. The next day my good friend Calvin, a hair stylist who owned two salons, one in Oakland and the other in San Jose, was closing the San Jose salon and asked me if I wanted the furniture for my salon. I could not believe it. Calvin sold me his furniture for next to nothing. When things like that happen, you know it's from God because it's good and perfect. The other great news was that I did not realize that the previous owner of the building had been there for over 30 years running a salon, and with me taking over the salon, I would get walk- ins from people who knew that this was previously a salon.

If there are dreams and goals you want to achieve, go out and do it! You can be your own worst enemy. I stepped out at 21 with no money and opened my salon. I took a risk, and I made $35,000 in my first year in business.

When I stepped out to start my breast cancer foundation in 2004, I was equally scared. I didn't know how I was going to solicit women going through cancer treatment. One day I saw a parent at my daughter's school who obviously was going through chemotherapy. I went to her and told her that I was starting a foundation for women going through treatment, and I wanted her to be my first recipient. She agreed to let me help her through my foundation and the rest is history. From that one service I was able to get my story out there and let people see what I was doing to help women feel and look good while going through treatment. If I had never asked this lady what she was going through, I would have never gotten the opportunity to work with a cancer patient and show the work that I was doing through my foundation. Sometimes you have to put your ego to the side in order to achieve greatness.

Acknowledgments

I have to acknowledge some key players in my life. I did not go through this journey alone; I had a village around me that supported me every step of the way. I am blessed to have you all in my life, and I love and appreciate you all!

Sherron, words cannot express how much I love you. I don't know my journey without you! We were mama's little angels and soldiers at the same time. You had to grow up fast to help raise me and Sedric, and for this I am eternally grateful to you for you being my sister. Thank you for always encouraging me and supporting everything I do, and thank you for always reminding me of my self- worth! I do listen to you. You will always and forever be the "boss of me".

Jaelyn, the day you came into my life, you changed me for the better. I was headed for destruction in a major way, I was so confused. You are truly a major blessing in my life. I wrote this book for you, I wanted you to know the good, the bad, and the ugly so that no one could ever tell you anything about me that you did not already know. I also wanted you to have the tools that I used to become unstoppable. Just in case I am not here on earth with you one day, you will have this book to read and follow. You have been right there with me every step of the way, and you watched me fall and saw me get right back up! It's called resilience! You are my greatest accomplishment, and I'm so proud of you. Keep God first and lean not into your own understanding. BE UNSTOPPABLE.

Sabrina, I love you so much. We did not live in the same house growing up, but thank God we had parents that kept us together no matter what. You were right there with me through the journey, and we made it out. I am so proud of you and the woman you have become. Let's create new possibilities!

Brely, thank you for being there for me on the days I was writing this book; reliving some of the stories I wrote about was not easy. Thank you for encouraging me, thank you for the mid-day prayer sessions, and overall thank you for just being available to me and giving me good, sound advice. You've been a part of my journey and you know the passion I have in my heart to help others. I am an UNSTOPPAPLE WATER WALKER!

Aunty Gwen, I know we don't always see eye to eye, but you know I love you! I have always been the one to challenge you and I think you secretly like that. I love you and appreciate you.

Uncle George, thank you for all of your continuous support in life. You helped me when I couldn't help myself, you were right there ever step of the way to my sobriety, not handicapping me but pushing me towards the finish line. Thank you, I love you.

Derrick Bedford, I love and appreciate Gregory Evans for life for introducing us. Thank you for the accountability meetings and talks; you are always being supportive to help others achieve greatness and I am so proud to know you. Your journey needs no introduction, it speaks for itself. Keep doing what you do! You and Cassie have a spiritual sister for life! Love you both!

Yolanda Denise, thank you for being there during my recovery, working with me throughout my personal development moments; it was quite a journey. You know everything I say, I say in love because I love you. Do not ever forget that you are the head and not the tail. God put you above and not beneath! NAMASTE!

Paula T, thank you for all you have done for me; you have been such a helper in my life wanting me to achieve nothing but greatness, and for that I appreciate you. Thank you for showing me the business side to the music industry. I am forever grateful for you in my life.

Jim Gardner, thank you for always making Pajama Studio my home. I appreciate all you have done for me, past and present.

Anthony Banks, thank you for trusting and believing in me when no else did. You were heaven sent. My discography in the music industry starts with you. I am grateful for the work we put in, and thanks to you I have worked with, and have been on some pioneer projects, with artists in the hip-hop music industry that paved the way for West Coast artists today. I'm proud to be a part of that history.

Kelsi Marie, you will always be my sister for life. God sent you to me when I needed Him most, and thanks to you being obedient, I now know the covering that goes around me when I give praise during the rough times. I am forever grateful! In addition, I am paying it forward by teaching others.

Otis Cooper, thank you for the motivation to keep going when I did not feel like I could. When it was time to record, I was being lazy and you pushed me to the point of making a great hit! Now it's "Easy Going" from here! Thank you and Tonette for your continuous support for me, I love you both!

BJ Kemp, thank you for being there for me throughout this project; I thank you for all that you do for me. Thanks for being a team player. I am so grateful to have you in my life - BMZ Kids for life!

Lynn Chess, thank you for being a light when I did not think it was possible. I will never forget when my mother was dying and you gave me the best advice that eventually sank in: *Take care of you, or you will be no good for your mother.* Whether you knew it or not, I had no choice but to get my life together after that conversation. I love you, Janie, and your whole family.

Aunty Carolyn, thank you for being there, whether it was a phone conversation or helping me with Jaelyn, I appreciate you for who you are in my life. I love you and **Uncle Carl** forever, my uncle and aunty!

Warren & Adriene Hogg, thank you Uncle and Aunty for being there, and thank you for your unwavering support! I love and appreciate you both.

Wendell & Lashawn Hogg, I love you uncle. Whether you know it or not you are my hero! Lashawn, thank you for taking excellent care of my uncle.

Fleetwood, Debra, Dwayne, and Rodney Irving, I'm blessed to still have my great uncles and aunt alive, love you.

To all of my cousins **Irving, Randolph, Cahee, Bailey, Douglas**, and **Foster cousins**! I love all of you! It's too many to mention! But you know who you are in my life!

BMZ, my church family. I love each and everyone of you.

Stacey Debono, thank you for taking this journey with me. This was my first book of many to come and I learned a lot during this process. Thank you for making this experience a wonderful one.

There were a lot of key players in my life growing up, so if I didn't mention your name, you know who you are. I love all of you and am grateful to have had you in my life. It takes a village and I truly had one growing up. I love you all!

Made in the USA
San Bernardino, CA
05 October 2018